CAMPING FOR CHRISTIAN YOUTH

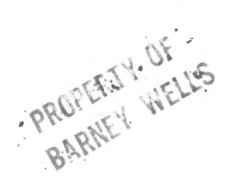

REVISED EDITION

Camping for Christian Youth

A GUIDE TO METHODS AND PRINCIPLES FOR EVANGELICAL CAMPS

FLOYD AND PAULINE TODD

BAKER BOOK HOUSE • Grand Rapids, Michigan 49506

Baker Book House

First Printing, April 1968
Second Printing, February 1971
Third Printing, November 1971

ISBN: 0-8010-8769-4

FIRST EDITION   F-N   LIBRARY OF CONGRESS CATALOG CARD NUMBER: 63-14972

FOREWORD

The late Saturday afternoon rain beat a tattoo on the roof as the young pastor maneuvered his car through a rugged pass of the Cascade Mountains—their spring beauty now rain-drenched.

Beside him his wife, holding the latest baby, spoke regretfully. "We should have had something to leave with them!"

"I know it!" the pastor agreed. "They want to have a boys' and girls' camp. They don't know the first thing to do. So . . . they invite me as conference camp director to come and meet with their new committee. We have less than an hour squeezed in after lunch and before the afternoon service to try to tell them how to organize and run a camp. Impossible!"

"But we couldn't have stayed later and made it home in time for our duties tomorrow."

"No, but in less than an hour how can you explain plans for a camp to a green committee—no matter how eager and cooperative?"

"You can't! And that's why we must have something to put in their hands the next time we are asked to help a new camp organize."

The sleeping baby was carefully deposited on the back seat. Out came paper and pencil. The windshield wipers clicked rhythmically as thoughts took shape on paper. The car crossed the divide, wending its way into one of the lush green valleys of Puget Sound. When the car stopped before the much remodeled wonder of a parsonage the young people called home, their rough draft was done—an organizational chart and plans for a boys' and girls' camp.

Thus, nearly two decades ago, this book was born, appropriately in some of the loveliest camp country in America. From this beginning the volume has grown along with the knowledge and experience of its authors. The first mimeographed leaflets gave a plan for organization and job descriptions of the denominational camp in the scenic Deception Pass region of Washington. In 1953, church leaders called Mr. Todd to Winona Lake, Indiana, headquarters to assume (among other duties) supervision of the denominational camping program for early youth. In response to urgent pleas, a camping manual was hurriedly prepared and published in early 1954 to help the many new camps being organized. This was enlarged and revised in 1957, still aimed toward helping Free Methodist camp committees organize new camps, though it has also been used as a text in some Bible colleges and institutions in camping courses within and outside of the denomination.

Now after more contacts by the authors with interchurch and secular camping groups, much study of camping literature, and visitation of camps across the continent, this edition is prepared for use in various evangelical groups. It contains much of the material found in the master's thesis of Mrs. Todd, "A Study of Resident, Evangelical, Summer Camping for Junior and Junior High Ages with Suggestions for Improvement in Methodology," presented to the Winona Lake School of Theology (Fuller Theological Seminary, Summer Session) in 1961. While the main focus of this volume is on camping for early youth (junior and junior high ages), it will give much material that is pertinent to camping for any age. It seeks to find by surveying the total camping movement in America the distinctive position of camping by evangelical groups.

The purpose of this book is triple: (1) to provide a text for Christian institutions for a survey course in camping, (2) to meet the needs of camp staffs and committees who desire over-all knowledge of evangelical camping, (3) to provide a text for a leadership and service training camping course in local churches and in camp staff training situations.

The authors have felt that writing this book has been an assignment from God, in return for the privilege He has given them of spending much time in the rewarding field of camping—in actual camp periods, in supervisory planning of a denominational camping program, and in presenting and attending workshops. Its ultimate aim is that His Kingdom may be advanced through improved camping practices in evangelical circles.

Winona Lake, Indiana   FLOYD AND PAULINE TODD

To our children
FLORA and RICH ALLEN
FREDA and BRUCE MCKEOWN
FRANKLIN

ACKNOWLEDGMENTS

Grateful appreciation is expressed particularly to Dr. Milford F. Henkel, professor of Christian education of the Winona Lake School of Theology. Under his teaching new vistas in philosophy and methodology of Christian camping were opening to the authors. Parts I and II contain some of his concepts. He critically read the entire typescript, giving valuable suggestions, as did also Rev. Richard Troup, former chairman of the NSSA Camp Commission and professor at Southeast Bible College, and Rev. Don Kinde, former chairman of the NSSA Camp Commission and head of camping in the Wesleyan Methodist Church.

To Mr. Graham Tinning, executive secretary of the Christian Camp and Conference Association, thanks is given for use of certain sections of this book which previously have appeared as articles in *Camp Life* (now renamed *Christian Camps and Conferences*), official organ of CAA. Copyrighted materials have generously been permitted use in this volume by the following publishers: American Camping Association, American Sunday School Union, Association Press, Baptist General Conference, Brethren Press, Burgess Publishing Company, Light and Life Press, McGraw-Hill Book Company, National Council of the Churches of Christ in the U.S.A., National Sunday School Association, W. B. Saunders Company, Standard Publishing Company, Recreation Magazine, and Westminster Press. Each selection so used is indicated by footnote.

I keep six honest serving-men
   They taught me all I knew;
Their names are What and Why and When
  And How and Where and Who.
       —Rudyard Kipling in *Just-So Stories*

CONTENTS

CHARTS

CAMPING FOR CHRISTIAN YOUTH

EVANGELICAL CAMPING

I. WHAT IS IT?

DEVELOPMENT — DEFINITION

WHAT IS AN EVANGELICAL?

Before evangelical camping may be defined, it is essential to define an evangelical.

In present-day American church life evangelicals are conservative Protestants. They are not "liberals," "modernists," or "neo-orthodox." Some total denominations and organizations are designated as evangelical. Other groups usually considered more liberal still have within their membership leaders who clearly proclaim their evangelical faith. Thus to be an evangelical does not necessarily mean affiliation with any particular body but acceptance of certain basic tenets of doctrine and practice.

Evangelicals take strong positive positions. They are evangelistic, seeking by "any means" to win men to a saving knowledge of the Lord Jesus Christ. Many evangelicals have joined to form the National Association of Evangelicals. Others are united under the American Council of Christian Churches in America. Many respect the accomplishment of the National Council of the Churches of Christ in the United States of America in certain fields but regret its actions in others. A number of evangelicals do not affiliate in any manner with this latter organization, but some continue to cooperate with it in some degree.

While it must be kept in mind that many evangelicals are not included organically in the National Association of Evangelicals, the latter's Statement of Faith probably best presents the doctrinal position of evangelicals in America, as the term is used in this volume:

1. We believe the Bible to be the inspired, the only infallible, authoritative Word of God.

2. We believe that there is one God, eternally existent in three persons, Father, Son, and Holy Ghost.

3. We believe in the deity of our Lord Jesus Christ, in His virgin birth, in His sinless life, in His miracles, in His vicarious and atoning death through His shed blood, in His bodily resurrection, in His ascension to the right hand of the Father, and in His personal return in power and glory.

4. We believe that for the salvation of lost and sinful man regeneration by the Holy Spirit is absolutely essential.

5. We believe in the present ministry of the Holy Spirit by whose indwelling the Christian is enabled to live a godly life.

6. We believe in the resurrection of both the saved and the lost; they that are saved unto the resurrection of life and they that are lost unto the resurrection of damnation.

7. We believe in the spiritual unity of believers in our Lord Jesus Christ.

1. THE DEVELOPMENT OF CAMPING

ROOTS OF CAMPING

Roots of camping may be considered to extend back to the dawn of human life. Some may wish to cite Adam and Eve as the first campers. Undoubtedly they were the first to learn "survival techniques" after their banishment from the Garden. Abram camped along the way as he led his troop westward. Later Moses for forty years was "camp director" for possibly the largest encampment in history, as the Israelites spent time in the wilderness in "trail camping"—family style. On the mountainside or along the shores of Lake Galilee Jesus, instructing His followers, set the pattern for present-day campers, who retreat to the out-of-doors to learn spiritual truths.

Some may wish to trace the beginnings of camping to the time when primitive man spent all his life outdoors. Others find traces of the distinctive elements of camping in succeeding historical epochs.

A thousand years before Christ, Egyptian groups were leaving their villages and cities to develop teamwork and improve health in the out-of-doors. Sparta strove to instill in her young men the ideals of self-discipline and physical fitness. The Athenians in their golden era encouraged a love of nature and development of aesthetic values.

Yet in spite of roots that span the centuries and center in other countries, the camping movement is uniquely American. With their dream of a new life of freedom, the Pilgrim fathers, before they left their flimsy vessel, recorded a meeting: "and so it was decided on the morrow that a small party would go ashore and select a camp site," and further, "a camp site was selected on high ground." [1] Settling on the rocky shores, these were actually campers, wresting from the unfriendly wilderness the necessities of life.

Those who followed the Pilgrims and the settlers at Jamestown, and those who pushed back the frontier, of necessity learned to

---

[1] L. B. Sharp, "The Role of Camping in Our American Heritage," *Camping Magazine,* February, 1942, p. 33.

camp, living off the land where they found themselves. The fur traders, the scouts, the wagon trains that later moved westward over the plains and mountain passes added to the image of outdoor living which is intertwined with American history. The Mexican War with its bivouacs, the Civil War with its encampments and its ballad "Tenting Tonight on the Old Camp Ground" added to the fervor for camping. The aura of adventure that has lingered from the days of the Indian with his tepee and campfire has tended to keep alive the love of outdoor living in American youth. Romantic ideas of camp life, overlooking the hardships and dangers of these days, have been imprinted in the consciousness of America. All are facets of the historical saga that has had its impact and made camping part of the American tradition.

BEGINNINGS OF CAMPING

Camping as a movement began during the Civil War. During these stirring times youth naturally was affected. Frederick William Gunn, head of the Gunnery School for Boys in Washington, Connecticut, earned for himself the title "Father of the American Camping Movement." He sometimes allowed his boys to drill and sleep out-of-doors like the soldiers. In 1861 this led to a two-weeks' summer encampment for his students at nearby Milford-on-the-Sound, where the boys worked, hiked, fished, and boated. He continued this summer school training (the first school camp) for his students until 1879.

In 1874 at Lake Chautauqua, New York, an out-of-door instruction center was opened by John Vincent and Lewis Miller. This had elements of camping, but later, as the "Chautauqua movement" that spread across America, it lost this aspect and became a cultural and social organization that employed some of the best lecturers and talent of the nation.

The North Mountain School of Physical Culture in Luzerne County, Pennsylvania, was the first private camp, a four-months' summer school in 1876. Dr. Joseph Trimble Rothrock, a physician of Wilkes-Barre, hoped to help frail boys to better health as they lived in tents, learning about nature, a consuming interest of the Doctor. Even though he charged $200 tuition, his camp was not financially profitable and was abandoned. But his attempt inspired others to similar endeavors.

Believing that the informality of camp living would break down barriers, Rev. George W. Hinkley in 1880 took seven of his church boys on a camping trip, the first church-sponsored camp. He realized his aim to know his boys better and influence them toward God. His program was one of religious instruction and evening services plus educational and sports activities. His first trip to Gardner Island, Wakefield, Rhode Island, led to his founding a home for boys at Hinkley, Maine.

Edmund Berkely Balch, concerned about the sons of wealthy parents idling away their summers at resorts, began Camp Chocorua on Asquam Lake in New Hampshire in 1880, the first camp with a program based on educational concepts. The boys wore uniforms of gray shorts and shirts with red belts, caps, and lacings. They were formed into four crews to work five hours each day at camp duties. Spiritual instruction was given and a chapel established. There were awards in tennis, sailing, swimming, diving, baseball, and for elements of good character. Two aims were to teach the boys responsibility to themselves and to others and to teach the dignity of work.

Organizational camping began in the YMCA, which in its early days had a strong evangelistic emphasis. Camp Dudley on Lake Champlain, near Westport, New York, is the oldest organized boys' camp still in existence. It is named for Sumner F. Dudley, who in 1885 took some YMCA boys on an eight-day fishing, swimming, and boating trip. Their camp was named "Camp Bald Head" because the boys had their heads shaved close before leaving on their trip. Later, after conducting several such camps, Dudley became a full-time YMCA worker, and the camp site he used is named in his honor.

Eventually there were those who had the idea that girls might profit from camping as well as their brothers. Professor Arey of Rochester, New York, loaned his Natural Science Camp for one month in 1891 for use by girls. In 1912 it became exclusively a girls' camp. In 1900 Elizabeth Ford Hold conducted the first private camp

CHART I. CHRONOLOGY OF EARLY ORGANIZED CAMPING

DATE	TYPE	FOUNDER	LOCATION	PURPOSE	PROGRAM
1861	First school camp	Frederick W. Gunn	Milford-on-Sound, Conn.	Occupy students during summer	Boating, hiking, sailing, fishing
1874	Beginning of Chautauquas	John Vincent, Lewis Miller	Chautauqua, N.Y.	Christian instruction center	Lectures, music, religion
1876	First private camp	Joseph Trimble Rothrock	North Mountain, Penna.	Help frail boys	Outdoor living, nature
1880	First church camp	Rev. George W. Hinkley	Wakefield, R.I.	Know boys, influence religiously	Religion, sports, education
1880	First private camp with special purpose	Ernest Berkely Balch	Asquam Lake, N.H.	Character education, teach dignity of work	Work, sports, awards
1885	First organizational camp	Sumner F. Dudley	Newburgh, N.Y.	Recreational	Boating, fishing, swimming
1892	First girls' camp	Professor Arey	Rochester, N.Y.	Natural Science Camp	
1912	First permanent church camp	John Alexander	Blue Galilee, Wis.	Auspices of International Sunday School Association	

for girls. Laura Mattoon in 1902 founded a camp expressly for girls, Camp Kehonka at Wolfeboro, New Hampshire.

While other religious leaders had sponsored camps before the date he cites, Peters gives the following account as the beginning of organized church camping:

The first permanent camping program sponsored by churches had its beginning at Lake Geneva, America's Blue Galilee, in Wisconsin in 1914. This date may be taken as marking the beginning of the religious camping movement in America. Mr. John L. Alexander, employed by the International Sunday-School Association, is credited with being the father of the religious camping movement. This movement was taken over by the International Council of Religious Education.[2]

FACTORS LEADING TO GROWTH OF CAMPING IN AMERICA

That camping as a movement is distinctly an American phenomenon is undisputed. The unique factors of American life that have given birth to this may be readily identified.

1. The first factor, already discussed, is the *heritage of American history*, which has cast a romantic aura around outdoor living.

2. In 1854, *Henry David Thoreau* wrote in *Walden* his reasons for seeking the out-of-doors. "I went into the woods because I wished to live deliberately, to front only the essential facts of life, and see if I could not learn what it had to teach, and not, when I came to die, discover that I had not lived. Our life is cluttered away by details. Simplify, simplify." These words became the call for his like-minded contemporaries and those that followed to break from tradition and the sophistication of mid-century living, seeking solace in the simple life. The intelligentsia of that day were strongly influenced, yet those who never read Thoreau also felt the impact of this revolt.

3. The *urbanization* and *industrialization* of America set the stage for increase in camping. In 1776, when the scattered colonies bravely declared themselves to be "the United States of America," only 2

[2] Raymond R. Peters, *Let's Go Camping* (Elgin, Ill.: Brethren Press, 1945), p. 13.

per cent of the population lived in cities or towns. The 1960 census reports that only 10 per cent live on farms and 36 per cent are classed as rural. This dramatic change in statistics is matched by as dramatic a change in living patterns.

4. Where once most children worked hard in the summer helping father and mother with farm tasks and preparation of the winter's food supply, now the majority are at leisure in the city. Because of *child labor* and *compulsory education laws,* city children have escaped the factories that once sought them.

5. A factor that has had a commanding effect on the growth of summer camping for youth is the *school calendar,* which dismisses the students for the summer. Camping has been a natural development to fill this leisure time of youth. If the movement for year-around public schooling continues to grow, it will pose a serious threat to camping as it is now structured.

6. The *increase in income* has been a spur to growth of camping. In early camping, the children of the rich attended private camps, and the children of the very poor, subsidized camps. Now camping caters also to the middle income group, the largest segment of society. As the members of this middle class have increased and as their incomes have risen to allow for more than the essentials, more of them have sent their children to camps.

7. Another factor in the popularity of camping is *America herself.* Her streams and lakes, her mountains and woodlands, her seashores and deserts issue their invitation to leave behind the cares and gadgets of modern life, to find in the out-of-doors the simplicity and verities of elemental living. Americans young and old are answering this call in increasing numbers.

"THE OLD-TIME CAMP MEETING"

Besides the influences and examples reflected in present-day church camping, another factor must be considered, especially in evangelical circles—"the old-time camp meeting," a family-style camp that contained many of the elements of true camping.

These revival-type, protracted meetings held outdoors with attendants camping on the site for extended periods are a religious phenomenon, distinctly American in origin. The first such meeting is reported to have been held in 1799 on the banks of the Red River in Kentucky. There hundreds were brought to repentance under the fervent preaching of Methodist and Presbyterian ministers. Through the years many such camps arose and flourished, with the Presbyterians gradually withdrawing. Baptists and Methodists dominated this field in the early part of the nineteenth century. The rise of revivalism in mid-century added impetus to the growth of the movement. "Brush arbor meetings" and camp meetings were widely attended by the common people.

Methodism itself began to look with disfavor on the excesses which sometimes occurred. But camp meetings were kept alive well into the twentieth century by interdenominational and Baptistic groups and the smaller Methodistic denominations.

These camp meetings paralleled the rise of organized camping, with an ultimate blending in some areas and groups. Because of their contribution to the total field of church camping the following expanded description is given from the personal experiences of the authors in the earlier years of this century.

Early camp meetings often shifted from one location to another each year. Sometimes such camps were used as means of starting new churches, with the evangelization of the surrounding community one of the conscious aims. More often they were held as times of spiritual renewal for pastors and laymen of the district. In either case attendance of residents nearby was solicited, and usually there was a good response in that more unhurried age.

The camp site was often the woods on a farm of one of the faithful, or a grove near town. Conveniences were few and facilities primitive. Outdoor privies were hastily constructed, and water was carried from a nearby well. Occasionally a community park was used that had better facilities.

The main tabernacle was of canvas, pitched the first day by sweating ministers and their conscripted sons. In the hot summer sun they stretched guy ropes, drove stakes, wove together the canvas sections. Campers arrived from all over the district at first in spring wagons, later in overloaded Model T's, Overlands, Studebakers, and Chevrolets. Every family had its own canvas tent, and usually each family did its own cooking.

Mother and the girls filled the straw ticks and made the beds on flat springs held off the ground by blocks of wood; then they arranged the dishes and food in the orange-crate cupboards and carried the water in tin pails. Father and the boys put up the tent, and Dad set up the small iron camp stove, while the boys gathered limbs or cut up logs for fuel.

Sometimes the women cooperated in communal cooking in a rough "cook shack." The discarded wood ranges, stoked from the huge woodpile, roasted the sheep or occasional quarter of beef provided by a sympathetic farmer. Sunday dinners were feasts with people from miles around coming with full baskets of delicacies, all put together in one extravaganza of food.

The camp program consisted of meetings only. At six o'clock in the morning the bell ringer walked through the camp swinging his handbell, calling the faithful to prayer in the tabernacle as he quoted an appropriate scripture: "Arise, the day is at hand. . . ." Those who might have tried to "sleep in" would have had little success considering the very vocal and emphatic praying in the tabernacle. After breakfast and family altar time in the tents, a "love feast" was held, with testimonies given as to God's dealings with individuals. Unforgettable are the memories of saints "getting blessed," walking the aisles, with hands upraised and countenances lighted, shouting praises to God for His blessings.

Following this the evangelist usually preached. In the afternoon again there was preaching service, often conducted by the ministers of the district. Required to sit through the long, sleepy afternoons on the plank benches, youngsters relieved their boredom as restless feet piled into hills and valleys the new shavings or straw which covered the tabernacle floor.

The climax of the day was the evening service, when a strong evangelistic message was presented, followed by a fervent altar call, which usually had a good response. As the saints gathered to pray with the repentant, it was an exciting and noisy time. There were dramatic changes in demeanor as weeping sinners experienced forgiveness. Conviction was deep; praying was lusty and unabashed; conversions were genuine and brought radically changed lives. Today's well-bred "acceptance of Christ" seems pallid in comparison.

(Yet, who can dictate the pattern that God is to use in changing lives?)

For children there was the morning "children's meeting" carried on by those who wished to see the needs of youth recognized. Most children were required to keep the rule of church "three times a day." There was no planned recreation for children or adults; this would have been considered sacrilegious. The concept was that camp meeting was a time set aside for advancing the Kingdom. An adult or young person might better be out in the woods in private (but not secret) prayer, carrying the burden for souls rather than thinking of his own pleasure. But children, being children even in those times, passed the time out of church making whistles of willow branches, carving walking sticks, climbing trees, meandering through the nearby woods, playing mumblety-peg, gathering hazelnuts and wild blackberries or strawberries.

In retrospect, the joy of camp meeting for a child was the friendships formed year after year with those who attended from across the conference, the adventure of outdoor living—sleeping with the night noises and only a thin canvas between oneself and the stars, and the deep consciousness that God was present on the grounds.

Actually this generation did a poor job of conserving their youth to the church. Many who knelt at the altar are far from the Church of Christ today. There was such a complete separation demanded and so little nurture given following conversion that only the spiritually strongest stayed true. Today's error may be the opposite: much nurture but not the insistence on separation and genuine conversion.

In the late 1920's and early 1930's the trend was to permanent camp grounds. Slowly but surely the pattern changed, but not without vigorous protest. Buildings soon replaced the tattered canvas tabernacles. Cabins replaced the family tents. Plumbing and wash-houses with showers replaced the privies and family washbasins. Meals began to be sold at the dining halls. Youth and children were provided with day-long activities. A camp store offered after-service refreshments. Study programs were provided. Grounds were beautified with lawns and shrubs, and placed under the watchful eye of full-time caretakers. Swimming pools began to appear. As the cultural pattern in the secular world changed, the old-time camp meeting became—for better or worse—a Bible conference.

With such a background, in denominations with camp-meeting traditions, boys' and girls' camps inevitably developed. As alert church leaders became familiar with the growth of secular camping, they realized that here was something that their churches could fit into their own tradition of camping.

Early church camp leaders in conservative circles were not without their critics. The authors vividly recall a prophecy given by one respected "old warrior of the Cross," who had traveled extensively in the denomination (though he knew of camping only by hearsay), "These boys' and girls' camps will be the ruin of the church."

Events have disproved his prediction. Church leaders who understand from actual experience what camping for early youth is accomplishing are generous in their praise of this agency of the church. They are quick to acknowledge that the stream of church life has been immeasurably enriched as year after year succeeding groups of youth have been won to and nurtured in things of God at camp.

Churches with or without this tradition of camp meetings are the richer to some extent for these early efforts at camping.

STAGES OF CAMPING

Students of the camping movement agree that organized camping has passed through a number of more or less recognizable stages during the last century. They further agree that these stages overlap and that there can be no clear line of demarcation between various camping periods.

Three different viewpoints will be presented: that of secular authorities, that of one who speaks for church camping in general, and that of evangelical camping leaders.

SECULAR CAMPING

Spokesmen for the American Camping Association use these designations for three periods of camping: (1) *the recreational stage,* (2) *the educational stage,* and (3) *the stage of social orientation and responsibility.*[3] Mitchell and Crawford date the three as follows: stage 1, 1860-1920; stage 2, 1920-30; stage 3, 1930 on.[4]

The *recreational stage* provided clean, healthful living in the great out-of-doors—an opportunity for underprivileged children to revel in nature, and for the children of wealth to learn how to use muscles in work and sports. Character education was an underlying aim, but this was to be absorbed by the campers without conscious planning as they mingled with their upright camp leaders. Competition, awards, and strict regimentation were common.

In the *educational stage* camps began consciously to meet the health, social, character, and educational needs of their campers. As progressive education was in its first vigor, with its emphasis on the individual need of the child, various expressive activities were introduced—dramatics, music, arts and crafts. Counselors, formerly chosen to give the campers a good time, now were better trained and were chosen on the basis of their skills.

The *social orientation and responsibility era* arrived as progressive education came into full bloom and knowledge of psychology, sociology, and teaching techniques increased. Camps became more self-conscious as studies revealed faults. Camping literature increased. One study of over one hundred camps indicated that the longer the camper stayed in camp, the poorer his physical condition became. As a result, camp tempo was slowed, and nurses and health staff were added. Small-group living and social adjustment assumed new proportions, with campers allowed to plan their own activities. The "democratic process" became important.

GENERAL CHURCH CAMPING

Clarice M. Bowman, who may be considered a spokesman for general church camping, accepts the first three stages as given above.

Four general stages in the growth of organized camping have been noted thus far—merging the one into the other, to be sure, but each ap-

[3] *Camp Counselor Course Outline* (Martinsville, Ind.: American Camping Association, 1962), p. 1.

[4] Viola Mitchell and Ida Crawford, *Camp Counseling* (Philadelphia: W. B. Saunders Company, 1961), p. 21.

parent now in the long look: the "rough-and-ready" stage of crude beginnings, usually with mass methods; the "educational" stage, taking
cognizance of individual differences and developing philosophies of education; the "increasing socialization" stage with the unit plan of buildings
and emphasis upon skills of group living; and now the "wilderness and
survival skill" stage.[5]

The survival stage which she notes can be observed even among
evangelical groups. It involves the newer technique in camping:
survival skills, canoe trips, wilderness camping. Devotees of this
trend feel that struggle with the elements is needed to counteract
the softness of modern life.

But Bowman also sees emergence of a possible fifth stage: one of
spiritual values.

. . . indications from many directions suggest that a possible fifth stage
may be one of spiritual values. While church leaders have been somewhat
relaxing their articulation of explicit spiritual emphases and training their
leaders in survival skills and the like, there has come—largely from non-
church camp groups—a ground swell of interest in incorporating more
definitely and more wisely some approach to religious or spiritual values.
This may be symptomatic of the spiritual hunger that seems apparent in
many quarters, even among those not noted for interest in pious matters.[6]

Evidence that this stage is emergent may be seen in the increased
number of articles on this subject in materials put out by the American Camping Association—the authoritative voice of organized
camping. In 1956 the Association incorporated into its standards
reference to spiritual values and it has a national committee at work
in this field.

Since consideration of "spiritual values" is a present-day trend, at
least in some camps, it is well to define what the term means in
secular, general church, and evangelical camping circles.

Secular camping literature gives these definitions:

. . . when I speak of the spiritual values in camping, I am not dealing
with the teachings of any religious group—Protestant, Catholic, or Jewish.
I am not thinking of any religious indoctrination program, nor of the

---

[5] Clarice M. Bowman, *Spiritual Values in Camping* (New York: Association
Press, 1954), p. 31.
[6] *Ibid.*, p. 32.

formal provisions which you may or may not make in your camps for worship. I am thinking rather of that deeper thing which is basic for all of us, the orientation of our souls toward God and toward our fellow men. . . . There are two major aspects to camp life which cause this to be true. The first is its closeness to nature. . . . There is another part of camp life which is just as rich in spiritual values. That is cooperative fellowship.[7]

Another writer states:

Spiritual values may be derived from experiences which are not related to the creed of a religion. A quiet moment spent watching the colors of the fire flare and recede, an exploratory walk in the green mysteries of a wooded hill, the singing of the camp song at the end of the day, all these contain attributes of spiritual values. They do not recognize nor need a religious creed. The Jewish boy in the New England camp may receive values similar to the Catholic in a Mid-Western camp or the Protestant boy in a Southern camp. The realization of these spiritual values is a religious experience designed to appeal to the intellect or to the "higher part of the mind," while at the same time it expresses a desire to act for or commune with an Infinite Being.[8]

Bowman, speaking again for *general church camping*, says, "By spiritual values is meant the orientation of persons Godward and toward others; these values are inherent in the very value of camping at its best."[9]

The *evangelical* speaking of spiritual values would probably give a much narrower definition. He would make a differentiation between spiritual values and aesthetic or social values. The secular writers include all three of these as spiritual—and they are in one sense. Evangelicals would probably say that a spiritual value in camping is *that which leads the camper to accept Christ as Saviour and enables him to walk more carefully as a born-again Christian.* They cannot divorce spiritual values from religious creed as does the more liberal church or secular camping literature. For the evangelical there is nothing new in emphasis upon such spiritual

[7] Lowell B. Hazzard, "Spiritual Values in Camping," in *Light from a Thousand Campfires* (New York: Association Press, 1960), p. 45.

[8] Mary Louise Mosely, "Help Campers Discover Enduring Basic Values," *Camping Magazine*, April, 1961, p. 22.

[9] Bowman, *op. cit.*, p. 40.

values in camping. Realizing these values has been a conscious aim from the beginning of evangelical camping.

The authors, in evaluating the fourth and fifth stages as given by Bowman, are inclined to classify them at present as trends rather than stages. In the years ahead they may become more dominant.

EVANGELICAL CAMPING

Dr. Milford Henkel, who teaches graduate courses in camping at Winona Lake School of Theology, Winona Lake, Indiana, is becoming recognized as a leader in evangelical camping and is a regular contributor to *Christian Camps and Conferences*, organ of the Christian Camp and Conference Association. His outline of the stages in camping is one he has modified from those given in Ward, *Organized Camping and Progressive Education.*[10]

The first stage is characterized by (1) indoctrination, (2) Bible study, (3) recreation, (4) evangelism. Ward observes that this was the pattern of the early YMCA camps. Many evangelical camps today are still of this pattern.

The second stage, which became prominent in organized camping following World War I, is characterized by (1) primitive conditions, (2) fixed curriculum, (3) awards, high competition, and influence of military competition, and (4) sports. At least two-thirds of present-day church camps are in either the first stage or the second or in a combination of the two.

The third stage, developed during the 1930's has as distinguishing features (1) democratic camp, (2) decision of campers as to program, (3) small groups, (4) social goals, (5) individual Bible study, and (6) continued evangelistic purpose. A few of these concepts have entered some of the evangelical camps.

The fourth stage is the one typical of many secular camps at present and is characterized by (1) a "democratic" religion (common truths not offensive to any faith), (2) no indoctrination, (3) a cooperative spirit, and (4) no evangelism. This stage is not seen in evangelical camps because it runs counter to their underlying concepts. Evangelicals desire their camps to be evangelistic and

[10] Carlos Edgar Ward, *Organized Camping and Progressive Education* (Arlington, Va.: Privately printed, 1935, out of print).

definitely strive to nurture their campers in Christian doctrine by precept and example.

PRESENT TRENDS IN CAMPING

GENERAL CAMPING

The American Camping Association gives the following listing of present-day trends in camping. Several of these points are applicable to church camping.

1. Rapid expansion; extension through day, trip, co-educational, family, public school camping, religious organizations, etc.
2. Local, state, and federal participation in camping programs.
3. Establishment of standards.
4. Increased leadership–training opportunities.
5. Emphasis on indigenous activities.
6. Increased publication of literature on camping.
7. Increased attention to camp planning.
8. Growth of professional opportunities.
9. Increased concern for health and safety.
10. Decentralization.
11. Flexibility in program.
12. Democratic planning.[11]

EVANGELICAL CAMPING

This outline is one used by the authors in camping workshops:

TRENDS IN EVANGELICAL CAMPING

I. Changing in Pattern from Conference to Camp

(See below, "Distinguishing Between a Camp and a Conference.") The change under consideration is responsible, at least in part, for the following trends now noticeable in evangelical camping:

A. *From Scheduled Activities to Decentralized Program*

The regimentation of day-long compulsory activities is being replaced by more choice for campers and more counselor-cen-

---

[11] *Camp Administration Course Outline* (Martinsville, Ind.: American Camping Association, 1961), p. 3.

tered activities. Few among evangelicals will accept the progressive education concept of day-long optional activities.

B. *Toward Better-Trained Personnel*

ACA requirements of three-day, on-site, pre-camp training are
met in few church camps, but a beginning is being made.

Counselor-in-Training (CIT) programs, in which older campers
receive in-camp training, are being developed in more church
camps.

Colleges and seminaries in evangelical circles are offering courses
in camping, with credit usually given in Christian or physical
education.

Through-the-year training is attempted by camp committees by
correspondence, required reading, and pre-camp workshops.

Church conventions include camping workshops and classes.

Leadership training courses in local churches offer credit toward
various certificates through courses in camping.

C. *Changing Concepts in Evangelism*

From mass evangelism the trend is toward more personal work
as better-trained counselors become available. Probably the ideal
is a combination of both.

D. *More Appreciation for the Naturalness of Environment*

Camp programs are tending toward utilization of the natural
elements in outdoor living and emphasis on appreciation of
nature.

II. Toward Coeducational Camping

The trend toward more coeducational camping in church groups,
although not evident in all areas and in all groups, is plainly discern-
ible. There are worthy arguments on both sides as to the value of
separate or mixed camping.

III. Toward More Camps for More Groups

Besides the traditional boys' and girls' and youth camps, all these and
more are coming into church circles: year-around camping, couples'
camps, family camps, week-end camping, trip camping, trail camping, day camping, camps for the handicapped, golden-age camping,
etc.

IV. Toward Better Camp Sites and Facilities

Camp committees are thinking bigger (and they should). The
standard of one acre per camper in buying camp sites is still far
from being reached in most instances, but progress is being made.

There is increased interest in meeting standards in facilities, safety, and sanitation.

V. Better Guidance

A. *Denominational*

Camping usually begins at the grass roots in a denomination, with headquarters finally "putting someone in charge" of a camping program that has sprouted while they were thinking of other things. Few evangelical churches have a camping division or even a director of camping. Much can be done and needs to be done in this field.

B. *Cooperative Efforts Among Evangelicals*

The National Sunday School Association Camp Commission and the Christian Camp and Conference Association have much to offer denominational and local leadership.

C. *Secular Camping Organizations*

Because of the rapid growth in church camping, secular camping organizations are recognizing the importance of church camping and seeking ways to help church groups improve camping practices.

EXTENT OF CAMPING

From its beginnings in New England, camping has grown continuously, reaching across the continent and into Canada. But since it is an individualistic movement with no central control, no way has been found to arrive at accurate statistics as to its growth and present extent. Only estimates may be made. Probably as authoritative a statement as may be found is one by Mitchell and Crawford, giving 1960 estimates.

It was a Yankee "notion" which, in the approximately hundred years since the birth of organized camping in 1861, has resulted in the establishment of an estimated 16,000-18,000 camps of different kinds serving from five to six million boys and girls each summer. It is estimated that about 12 per cent of youngsters in school now enjoy an experience at some camp during the summer. Boys outnumber girls about two to one and the majority of campers range in age from nine to fourteen years.

About 15,000 persons find year-round occupation in camping while an additional 175,000 or more are added to the peak camp season; the majority of the latter are college graduates or college students seeking re-

CHRISTIAN CAMPING, A FILMSTRIP PROGRAM

This filmstrip series, planned by the authors, was produced by Cathedral Films in response to the requests of Christian camping agencies which were experiencing a mushrooming growth of church-related camps. The filmstrip series serves as a companion piece to this book, and is most useful in introducing and promoting the benefits of Christian camping to others, as well as providing training and instruction for camping leaders and camp committees.

Graham Tinning, executive director of Christian Camp and Conference International, served as consultant during production of the series. Outstanding leaders in the field of Christian camping reviewed and criticized scripts before production began.

The complete set of four full-color filmstrips, two records, introductory study guide, four comprehensive study guides, all in a full-color storage box, sells for $30.60. Each filmstrip, with a study guide, sells for $7.00. The record is $3.00. The record pairs are: Objectives/Administration and The Counselor/The Program. Running time is fifteen minutes for each filmstrip.

A résumé of the content of each filmstrip follows on the next page.

1.
OBJECTIVES
In Christian Camping

Camp Director Dick, in opening scenes, attempts to sell a church board on the values of camping. Reluctant board members are not easily persuaded, but Dick presents an overwhelming case for Christian camping.

2.
ADMINISTRATION
In Christian Camping

The Camp Committee selects Dick as Camp Director. His numerous duties are presented and patterns are unfolded for efficient camp administration. The administrative staff members are introduced and their contributions to the practical and spiritual ministries of the camp are highlighted.

3.
THE COUNSELOR
In Christian Camping

Camp Director Dick prepares for the arrival of the camp staff for the pre-camp training sessions. Andy, a first-time counselor, appears, and training sessions are prepared as Andy learns camping techniques and skills and receives spiritual preparation for his camp ministry.

4.
THE PROGRAM
In Christian Camping

Camp Director Dick speaks to a college camping class. He shows the pattern for establishing a camp program consistent with its objectives — determining camp objectives, selecting program pattern, considering program principles, and choosing program elements.

munerative employment for the summer. The camps themselves vary greatly in size, some having as few as eight campers while others accommodate over 1,000. The average, however, probably handles from eighty-five to 125 campers.[12]

Today throughout most denominations and religious youth movements camping is a burgeoning movement. Each year sees the beginning of new church camps. In fact, camping is becoming such an accepted part of church life that religious camping now dominates the camping field.

Statisticians tell us that the number of individual boys and girls attending summer camp sponsored by religious groups is now greater than the attendance at all other camps put together.[13]

It would be a long and difficult task to determine the number of children that attend camps under Christian auspices of either a church, or a denomination. One rather sketchy study made of Christian camping in the United States based on the definition of Christian camps including the YMCA and YWCA camps along with all the churches and denominations estimated that there were over two million campers under these auspices. With this figure as a basis it would seem safe to assume that there are a total of somewhere in the neighborhood of four million children and young people who attend camp under church or secular leadership.[14]

Many of the first camps were begun by evangelical organizations such as the YWCA and YMCA, yet camping was slower to begin in evangelical churches, because of their inbred conservatism. However, as they realized that camps constitute an effective arm of evangelism, their sponsoring of camps increased at a rapid rate.

There are no statistics available on the growth of camping in evangelical circles, yet the establishment of numerous new camps and the enlargement of existing camps indicates a rapid growth. . . . At any rate, it is probable that camp attendance in evangelical circles is higher than any other.[15]

---

[12] Mitchell and Crawford, *op. cit.*, p. 8.

[13] Maurice D. Bone, "Church Sponsored Camping," *Recreation*, March, 1961, p. 126.

[14] *Philosophy of Christian Camping* (Chicago: National Sunday School Association Camp Commission, 1962), p. 2.

[15] *Ibid.*

A study by the NSSA Camp Commission for the 1961 camp season gives the estimate of nearly 500,000 resident campers of all ages in its affiliated bodies.[16]

2. DEFINITION OF CAMPING

It was in 1916 that President Charles W. Eliot of Harvard University made his famous statement that "the organized summer camp is the most important step in education that America has given the world." Since that time there have been many who would concur. What he saw in its infancy has grown prodigiously, developing unexpected facets.

What is the composition of this social and educational phenomenon that has become such an accepted element in American life?

CLASSIFICATION OF CAMPS

In studying the nature of camping it is well to consider first the types of camping and camps which may be found in America today.

Distinction here must be made between "organized camping" and "informal camping"—the latter showing as rapid an upsurge as the former in the past decade. The main purpose of informal camping

[16] As used in this book, the terms "junior" and "junior high" refer to the age-groups 9, 10, 11 and 12, 13, 14, respectively.

by families and groups is to have a family or group enjoy an outing together in the out-of-doors. One need only visit a state or national park on a week end in summer to discover the growing popularity of this back-to-nature movement. National and state governments cannot keep pace with the demand for public camping facilities. Down sleeping bags and quickly erected tents are becoming new status symbols for American families, and seemingly the family without a camping adventure to relate has little to talk about among many of its contemporaries.

Recognizing the implications of this type of camping, the American Camping Association has concerned itself with a division of family camping, anticipating a full organizational structure in this field.

It is not with informal camping that this volume is concerned, however (intriguing as a study of it might be), but rather with organized camping.

There are several camping classifications, varying with their authors. The following has been arranged to the satisfaction of the writers of this volume.

TYPES OF CAMPS

I. Classification by sponsorship
   A. Organizational and agency
   B. Private
   C. Public
   D. Religious

II. Classification by groups served
   A. Early youth
     1. Junior
       a. Boys
       b. Girls
       c. Coeducational
     2. Junior high
       a. Boys
       b. Girls
       c. Coeducational

   B. Senior high and "teen camps"
      1. Boys
      2. Girls
      3. Coeducational
   C. Family
   D. Adult
      1. Young adult
      2. Couples
      3. Golden age
      4. Men's retreats, etc.
   E. Groups with special needs
   F. Groups with special interests
III. Classification by time and place
   A. Resident
      1. Long-term
      2. Short-term
      3. Week-end
   B. Day
   C. Trip and Trail

In describing any camp one should take a designation from each of the above three groupings: for example, "a long-term resident, private camp for junior high girls," or "an agency, coed day camp for juniors," or "a week-end, resident, family camp."

CLASSIFICATION BY SPONSORSHIP

Organizational or agency camps are those operated by non-profit private organizations: Boy Scouts, Girl Scouts, Boys Clubs of America, YMCA, YWCA, settlement houses, and other such social agencies. They are supported in part by the public through United Fund or private subscription. Hence their camp fee is low, averaging two to four dollars a day, with many camperships available for needy youth. Since they are usually a continuation of a year-round program, and because they must accommodate many campers during the season, they are likely to be short-term camps. Most of the staff are salaried, but there are some volunteers. Often camps for persons with special needs, such as the mentally retarded, etc., are agency camps.

Private or commercial camps are those sponsored by private individuals who desire to operate with a profit. Fees are consequently high, usually between fifty and one hundred dollars weekly, though reportedly one ministering to an especially wealthy clientele charges two hundred dollars per week. Such camps are generally long-term, often not accepting registrations for less than four or even eight weeks. Competition to secure campers keeps their standards high. Staffs are paid, and facilities may be elaborate, or there may be an elaborately preserved "ruggedness." Each camp tries to be distinctive in emphasis. Some camps offer music, drama, art—even horseback riding or baton twirling—as their specialty. The Association of Private Camps (see address in Appendix) makes a contribution not only to its own membership but to camping in general through its research and educational programs.

Public (tax-supported) camps include those operated by municipalities, state and national parks, governmental agencies, and schools. Because of their public support, fees are usually low; many are day camps. School camping or "outdoor education" is having a rapid growth, with several states experimenting in it. Its purpose is to extend the benefits of camping to more public school children. Usually expenses are met from school funds except that children furnish or pay for their own food. Regular teachers compose the staff, camping with the students. The philosophy is to "learn by doing" and to present those learning experiences which can best be taught out of the classroom. Because of its implications for other types of camping, every thoughtful student of camping should observe public school camping.

Religious or church camping is sometimes classified with organizational camping. However, it is becoming such a burgeoning movement and has such a distinctive format that it deserves a separate category. While slower to begin in camping than some other groups, evangelical churches have in the last decade made up for lost time with a rapid rate of growth. Again, because their camping program is usually a continuation of a year-around ministry, the camps are usually short-term, the average length being one week. Fees are low because of subsidies in the form of volunteer staff. members, free camp sites, and often direct contribution from the sponsoring bodies. In the past few years there has been a growing concern with meeting better camping standards. Protestant denominations, interdenominational youth groups, the Salvation Army, Jewish welfare groups, and Catholic youth organizations are included in this category.

CLASSIFICATION BY GROUPS SERVED

Camps for early youth ordinarily include children in grades four through nine; they may be either coeducational or for each sex separately. Most church groups have boys and girls together at this age. Agency camps are moving toward coeducation, but probably the majority are still separate.

Senior high and teen camps in churches are usually coeducational, with separate camps for the sexes held most frequently by organizational camps.

Family camping to strengthen family ties is on the increase in church circles; programs provide for all-family participation as well as graded activities. Some agency camps are also sponsoring family camping.

Adult camping is rapidly expanding in both church and secular groups. It includes young adult camps, usually coeducational; couples' camps, when the children are left at home and young married couples become reacquainted; golden-age camping for senior citizens; men's week-end retreats; and other special groupings.

Persons with special needs are usually ministered to by organizational groups. The diabetic, mentally retarded, deaf, crippled, socially maladjusted, undernourished, etc., have camps designed to meet their special needs. Some church groups are also entering this field.

Groups with special interests are usually served by private camps. Music, art, sports, work projects, ranching, or tutoring in some specialty is the primary emphasis.

CLASSIFICATION BY TIME AND PLACE

Resident camps are those in which the campers eat, sleep, and live twenty-four hours a day (with possible off-site trips occasionally) on the camp site. Although the American Camping Association defines short-term camps as those of five days or less, the authors use this term as descriptive of the usual camp in evangelical circles, which averages one week. Short-term church camps may last from one to two weeks or be as brief as five or six days. Long-term camps are usually from four to eight or ten weeks. Week-end camping is becoming popular especially in church circles and among other groups that have year-around camping facilities. Private camps are majoring in winter sports in week-end camping, such as "ski camps."

Day camps are usually held in metropolitan or city areas. Children arrive right after breakfast, bring their lunch or the materials with which to prepare it, and go home usually before the evening meal. Their day's activities include everything possible from regular camping procedures. Scouts, YMCA, YWCA, and 4-H are especially active in this field, and more churches are entering it. Most municipal camps are day camps.

Trip or trail camping needs no special camp site. This is usually "wilderness camping." Provisions must be made for living off the land with little equipment except what is carried on one's back or mount, or in a canoe. This type of camping should be restricted to older youth or adults. It is often a privilege allowed campers already enrolled in a resident camp.

GENERAL DEFINITIONS OF CAMPING

Camp has been defined in both brief and verbose manners. One of the most succinct definitions is the one by Robert Rubin, who characterizes camping as "communal living close to nature with a set purpose." [1]

In a more specific way Hedley S. Dimock lists the elements of organized camping:

The characteristic elements that, blended together in the right proportion, constitute an organized camp include (1) persons, (2) outdoor living, (3) living in groups, (4) a camp community, (5) leadership and conditions designed to satisfy personal needs and interests and to stimulate wholesome personal, social and spiritual development. [2]

[1] Robert Rubin, *The Book of Camping* (New York: Association Press, 1949), p. 1.
[2] Hedley S. Dimock, *Administration of the Modern Camp* (New York: Association Press, 1957), p. 22.

The American Camping Association gives the following as a general definition of camping:

> Organized (Resident, Day) Camping is an experience in group living in a natural environment. It is a sustained experience under the supervision of trained leadership. Camping provides a creative, educational experience in cooperative group living in the outdoors. It utilizes the resources of the natural surroundings to contribute significantly to mental, physical, social, and spiritual growth of individual campers.[3]

Many secular camp leaders are greatly concerned lest camping lose its "real" quality. Articles labor the theme "Let's put camping back into our camps." Hence it is profitable to know what secular camp authorities consider "real camping."

A former president of the American Camping Association, Barbara Ellen Joy, states:

> If we delve back into early accounts of camps and camping, we find the natural activities inherent in the camp environment constituted the camp program. . . . Then gradually . . . camping which should be simple, adventuresome living in the outdoors, had become a very complicated and high-powered enterprise. Now the wheel is turning and we are again trying to go back to a simple, unelaborate, unaffected, natural, and sound way of outdoor living.

.   .   .   .   .

> What, then, is "real camping," this "will o' the wisp" which seems to be eluding us? Briefly, it is the utilization of the fullest extent compatible with camp objectives—which will vary with the type and needs of campers in each camp—of the interests, the needs, the potentialities which are inherent in the camp situation. It means doing and discovering things. It means handling objects, and using materials which are right there on the camp location or easily accessible. It means that the children participate in indigenous activities rather than in activities brought in from the outside.[4]

[3] *Camping Is Education* (Martinsville, Ind.: American Camping Association, 1960), p. 8.

[4] Barbara Ellen Joy, *Camping* (Minneapolis: Burgess Publishing Company, 1957), p. 5.

Dimock suggests that the program of an organized camp consists of the "experiences that are indigenous to group living in the out-of-doors setting." [5] He indicates that it is this indigenous element that is the heart of "real camping" and makes it different from a conference, an athletic event, or any other type of group gathering.

DISTINGUISHING BETWEEN A CAMP AND A CONFERENCE

Before attempting to explore definitions of church camping, it is pertinent at this point to discover the differences between a camp and a conference.

Some people feel that a camp is for children, a conference for adults. But there are fundamental elements in one that contrast with those in the other. The following list of elements has been worked out by students at Winona Lake School of Theology in a camping course under the guidance of Dr. Milford F. Henkel:

A Church Camp	*A Conference*
Leisurely pace	Fast-moving
Simple, relaxed life	Designed for inspiration
Controlled environment	Less controlled environment
Small-group activity	Mass activity
Counselor centered	Platform centered
No "prima donna" as speaker	Expert speakers
Better-trained counselors	Counselors mainly disciplinarians
Simple outdoor setting	Often elaborate facilities
Nature emphasis	Nature only incidental
Emphasis on personal evangelism	Mass evangelism
Informal worship	Formal worship
Personal counseling	Group instruction
Individual worship stressing private devotions	Mass approach to worship
Development of the individual	Leadership training
Informal program	Formal program
Participation by all	Spectator status for most

[5] Dimock, *op. cit.*, p. 22.

Using the above topics, directors of twenty-four Free Methodist camps were asked to analyze their camps. They marked the elements characteristic of a camp, those typical of a conference, and those common to both that were used in their own camp programs. After the workshop in which this study was made, results were tabulated.

Elements in 24 Free Methodist Camps

Like a camp	28% of total elements listed
Like a conference	44% of total elements listed
Like both	28% of total elements listed

or stated differently

Like a camp	56%
Like a conference	72%

From this study it is easy to see that camping elements in this denomination are pretty well overshadowed by the convention atmosphere, probably because most of them have evolved from the camp meeting, which has today become a Bible conference. Several directors stated their desire to see more true camping elements in their camps.

But not all evangelical church groups are concerned about having true camps. They consider the indoctrination and evangelization of their youth more important than teaching how to char a potato in coals or to sleep in a bumpy bough bed.

The American Sunday School Union states frankly that camping is not its aim. In fact, it prefers to call its summer camps "Bible conferences."

Because the buildings are sometimes rustic log cabins, situated in a secluded wooded setting, and because such activities as hiking, camp-fire services, and other outdoor activities are a part of the program, these gatherings are sometimes called camps. However, we feel that the Bible emphasis is the distinguishing feature. Unlike the Scouts and similar organizations that feature camping activities, we like to think of our summer gatherings as Bible Conferences. That is, instead of placing the emphasis on camping, as such, with all the associated activities as outdoor cooking, nature studies, and handcraft (which are all good), we place the emphasis on Bible training and spiritual growth all in an atmosphere of the great out-of-doors.[6]

Among evangelical church groups few attempt to carry on camping as indicated in the list of characteristics of camping given previously. One of the greatest drawbacks for evangelical church camps in furthering small-group camping is the necessity for well-trained counselors. Also many evangelicals do not wish to give up efforts at mass evangelism or formal classes. Some reject this pattern of camping because they feel it follows too closely the pragmatic philosophy of progressive education, which will be discussed later. Probably the majority of evangelical camps are somewhere between camp and conference, endeavoring to inject as much "real camping" as possible in their program while retaining the aspects of conference programming considered essential.

DEFINING GENERAL CHURCH CAMPING

Church camping as a particular phase of the camping movement must have its own distinctive definition, which varies with the person giving it. Anyone attempting to define church camping should do so only after studying the materials presented in the first part of this chapter. Then, knowing the nature of camping, its classifications, what is "real camping," the difference between a camp and a conference, he is ready to decide the meaning of camping for himself or his organization.

The following definition of camping is given by the Special Committee on Camps and Conferences of the International Council of Religious Education.

Church camping is characterized by an actual experience of living out-of-doors. Simple living in natural surroundings provides environment conducive to the development and practice of the Christian spirit. In this setting countless ways are afforded the camper to deepen his understanding of God's Word and His purposes.

The twenty-four-hour-a-day experience provides opportunities for Christian community living. Through group living, intimate relationships

[6] "Bible Conference Echoes," *The Sunday School Missionary,* January-March, 1959, pp. 1, 2.

between camper and Christian counselor create excellent situations in which the camper is helped to understand and practice the teaching of Jesus.

The church camp is a situation away from home providing numerous growing-up experiences for boys and girls. For persons of all ages it gives a new perspective with regard to the individual home, church, and community.

The conscious effort to establish a Christian community offers unique opportunities for Christian growth and for each camper to take the next step in his personal religious decisions.[7]

While this is a description rather than a definition, it presents the non-conservative point of view. It is significant in its omission of specific emphasis—as might be expected—on taking Christ as a Saviour in a personal experience.

ARRIVING AT A DEFINITION OF EVANGELICAL CAMPING

An excellent definition from the evangelical viewpoint is this one by Ethel Ruff Mattson:

WHAT IS CAMP?

A *place* where campers become aware in a new and beautiful way of the presence of the Creator as they see Him behind the beauties of nature.

A *plan* where Christ is brought out in every element of the program.

An *experience* whereby old lives are made new by the power of the Lord Himself, manifested in the lives of the campers.

A *solution* to problems that only can be solved in actual life situations rather than in formal teaching situations.[8]

In a rough draft of a paper on the philosophy of camping prepared by a committee on the National Sunday School Association Camp Commission this definition is given of evangelical camping:

Christian camping may be defined as *an experience in Christian living in the out-of-doors under guidance*.

[7] *Toward Better Church Camping* (Chicago: Special Committee on Camps and Conferences, International Council of Religious Education, 1950), p. 5.
[8] Violet C. Carlson, *The Christian Educator's File* (Chicago: Moody Press, 1954), p. 29.

The phrase *experience in Christian living* assumes both individual experience and experience as a member of a group, be that group one's peers or many ages, as in a family camp. It also presupposes that this experience in Christian living is more than instruction in how to live as a Christian but is primarily an opportunity to practice one's Christian principles in a "laboratory" under guidance. The phrase *in the out-of-doors* signifies more than simply being in the open air. It carries with it the connotation of being away from civilized life with enough space to permit learning skills related to getting along in the out-of-doors. It should be a setting conducive to developing appreciation of the natural world and its Creator. The term *under guidance* has special reference to the fact that campers are away from home and under the supervision of trained persons (counselors). It is this freedom from ordinary distractions of usual routine and independence from parental influence that permits campers to concentrate on important issues, spiritual as well as other personal ones.[9]

The following brief definition has been arrived at by the authors for presentation in workshops for camp directors: "Christian camping is a Christ-centered program of small-group living in a simple, controlled out-of-door environment where the camper is enabled to develop recreational, educational, and social skills and to know Christ as Saviour and Friend."

All churches consider camping to be a part of their over-all program of Christian education. *But evangelical camps are frankly evangelistic in nature. Their supreme and conscious aim is to see each camper won to Christ in a definite, personal, religious experience whether it be in a public service, in a private counseling session, or alone in a quiet woods. This evangelistic urge is a basic and distinctive ingredient in evangelical camps; without it a camp is not evangelical.*

Camping has many facets. No one definition will encompass all its diverse elements. There is need for tolerance. What is camping for one need not be despised by another. Each should be free to let the great idea of camping assume its own form within the confines of his organizational pattern.

---

[9] *Why Are We Camping?* Report of the Committee on Christian Camping Philosophy (Chicago: National Sunday School Association, 1960), pp. 7, 8.

BIBLIOGRAPHY

The following books for further study in the field of camp development and camp definition have been arranged under each heading in recommended order of purchase for the average evangelical camp. See bibliographies listed in Appendix for further related publications.

CAMP DEVELOPMENT

Mitchell, Viola, and Crawford, Ida B. *Camp Counseling.* Philadelphia: W. B. Saunders Company, 1961. $6.25.

CAMP DEFINITION

Camp Commission, National Sunday School Association. *Guiding Principles for Christian Camping.* Chicago: The Association, 1962. 50¢. (Evangelical in emphasis.)

Webb, Kenneth B. (editor). *Light from a Thousand Campfires.* New York: Association Press, 1960. $4.95.

Camping Is Education. Martinsville, Ind.: American Camping Association, 1960. 75¢.

Johnson, C. Walton. *The Unique Mission of the Summer Camp.* Martinsville, Ind.: American Camping Association, 1960. 75¢.

Lyle, Betty. *Camping, What Is It?* Martinsville, Ind.: American Camping Association, 1947. 30¢.

STUDY HELPS

1. Define an evangelical, positively and negatively.
2. Name and describe some of the early camps.
3. What factors in American life assisted in growth of organized camping?
4. What elements of "real camping" were found in the "old-time camp meeting"?
5. Name and describe the three stages in secular camping.
6. How do secular and evangelical leaders differ in defining spiritual values?
7. What are Henkel's four stages of camping?
8. What are five present-day trends in evangelical camping?
9. How does camping in evangelical circles compare with that in other groups?
10. Give four classifications of camps by sponsorship; five by groups

served. Distinguish between resident and day camping.
11. What is meant by "real camping" as defined by secular camping authorities?
12. Name ways in which a camp differs from a conference.
13. What is the distinctive element that makes a camp evangelical?

PROJECTS

1. Write a history of the camp in which you are most interested.
2. Rate this camp as to whether it is more like a camp or a conference.
3. Write an original definition of camping according to your philosophy.

II. WHY DO IT?

PHILOSOPHY — OBJECTIVES

"But that isn't camping!" She said it emphatically, with a disdainful wave of her hand that made her cigarette suddenly glow—this pert, self-assured representative of an agency camp.

It was in a workshop on coeducational camping at a secular camping convention. The moderator, a camping authority from a liberal denomination, had gathered the attendants of the workshop in an informal circle and was encouraging each to contribute items of interest about his own camp.

A Bible-loving Lutheran told of the classes in Bible study which were among the activities scheduled for his camp.

This caught the attention of the agency representative. Unbelievingly she asked, "You mean you have scheduled classes in Bible study?" Then followed her contemptuous *"But that isn't camping!"*

"Isn't it?" asked the Lutheran, on the defensive. "It is where I come from."

The moderator suavely explained to the unreceptive Lutheran how much better it would be, rather than formally teaching the catechetical truth that "God is Creator of all things," to provide experiences for the child to observe nature. Then, after seeing these natural wonders, the child would discover for himself and exclaim in awe, "God must have made these." The watchful counselor would quote an appropriate Bible verse and confirm the camper in his self-discovery. "Ah," said the moderator, "that is true learning!"

After the session broke up, evangelicals gathered around the Lutheran, assuring him, "Brother, we're on your side."

In the face of such criticism, what should evangelicals do? They may either bristle up and harden their determination to do things the way they are doing them, no matter what, or, conversely, begin to doubt their own methods in the face of the polished confidence of exponents of pragmatic camping theories.

What is needed is a clear concept of the forces at work in the field of philosophy of education which have shaped methods in both modern and evangelical camping during the past decades.

3. DEVELOPING AN EVANGELICAL PHILOSOPHY OF CAMPING

Listing of goals and objectives in camping is a common practice in both secular and religious camping literature. The goals are actually the outgrowth of certain broad philosophic concepts held by the formulator of the goals. Few perhaps have probed deeply enough to realize this. These basic beliefs become so much a part of one that probably few people—other than those interested in the study of philosophy—have put them into words.

Yet because evangelicals believe that out of these concepts come objectives and out of objectives comes methods, it is important that camp directors be aware of the implications of the concepts.

In the camping field now there are two contrasting philosophies of education which result in two different methods of camping.

PRAGMATIC CONCEPTS

The agnostic, pragmatic system of philosophy has come on the scene during this century with a powerful, but perhaps too little understood, impact on all of American life. Progressive education has permeated teachers' colleges and has all but taken over the public educational system. A very general statement of pragmatic concepts, as expounded by its leader John Dewey in his book *Democracy and Education*,[1] is summarized here. Not all pragmatists would agree with every one of these statements.

1. There is no God, hence no Absolute Truth, nor any unchanging, lesser absolute truths. There is no reality, nor is any theory of reality necessary. What works is true; if religion works for you, it is true for you.

2. Education should not have fixed, unchanging aims, but if it has one, it is striving for social efficiency—the adjustment of the individual to his environment.

3. Education is obtained only by living or experiencing truth, not

[1] John Dewey, *Democracy and Education* (New York: The Macmillan Company, 1916).

by formal instruction. Since the pupil learns only what he experiences and only that for which he has a "felt need," the project, problem-solving, and scientific methods are valid.

4. Any curriculum must be child-centered, not subject-centered, nor ideal-centered (nor, of course, God-centered). If it does not stem from the present needs of the child, it is useless. Those things which are socially most fundamental are most important.

5. There is no fixed moral code. Moral truths for each generation must be worked out by themselves to fit their own needs.

6. There is no authority except life itself. Social situations must not be autocratically controlled but resolved through group action.

THE PRAGMATIC CAMP

Obviously the camp director holding this philosophy will have a camp that matches his thought patterns. The extreme pragmatist will plan his camp as follows:

1. Because there is no fixed body of truths, everyone must work out his own religious beliefs. There is no set religious instruction, though a quiet time may be encouraged when each one is to approach Deity in his own manner (or think good thoughts). Evangelism is discouraged.

2. Social efficiency is considered the all-important aim. In order to reach this, small-group living is encouraged. The adjustment of the camper to his group and development of social qualities are paramount values.

3. There are no formal classes. Small groups do as they decide among themselves. The counselor does not suggest projects but helps the groups realize their "felt needs" for that day. There are few or no scheduled activities other than those that meet physical needs.

4. The curriculum emphasizes the self-expression of the camper—in outdoor living, drama, creative writing, crafts, etc.

5. Ideals of conduct must not be arbitrarily taught, but campers will be led to discover some for themselves in casual situations during everyday occurrences.

6. The camp is "democratic." Authority is vested in the campers themselves as far as possible. Good behavior is obtained through

pressure of group approval. The counselor is non-autocratic, making no arbitrary decisions but leading the group to make its own decisions.

EVANGELICAL CONCEPTS

Not all evangelicals will accept the following in all its points, but in general it may be considered an accurate statement of evangelical philosophic concepts.

1. There is a God who is Absolute Truth and Absolute Reality, unchanging. There is a lesser, fixed body of truths to be passed on to succeeding generations.

2. There should be formalized education. The evangelical takes seriously the injunction of the Shema, "and thou shalt teach [these words] diligently unto thy children . . ." (Deut. 6:7).

3. The final aim of education is adjustment to God. (This does not rule out a crisis experience in salvation which involves more than education.) The Christian needs to learn social values, but he is instructed, "be ye not conformed to this world: but be ye transformed" (Rom. 12:2). Christ did not adjust to His environment but triumphed over it.

4. Curriculum should be Christ-centered, child and Word related. Each has its place in the teaching process.

5. There is a fixed moral code based on God's immutable precepts that must be taught to youth.

6. God is the Supreme Authority, but He shares this authority with parents, church, and civil leaders. The authority is based on love which is just, firm, sympathetic.

THE EVANGELICAL CAMP

With this background of philosophic thought, how does the evangelical plan his camping program? First, he does not "throw out the baby with the bath water." He categorically rejects agnostic pragmatism as a philosophy. But he may with profit use some of the methods of John Dewey, who must be acknowledged as a pedagogical scientist. However, it should also be noted that Dewey did not originate all the methods he advocated but borrowed heavily from former educators. Hence the evangelical may use methods of progressive education when they fit in with his over-all philosophic pattern, rejecting those which conflict.

The evangelical camp may include these elements:

1. It will include a definite religious pattern consistent with the religious emphasis of its sponsors.

2. There is a fixed body of truths to be passed on to youth. Different means will be used, including both formal and informal classes. "Formal classes" means Bible classes, definite instructional periods, and large-group meetings.

3. Definite goals to be achieved will be formulated before camp opens and will give direction to the entire program. These goals will be reinterpreted in the light of the need of individual campers and staff during the camping period.

4. Since ultimately all education is adjustment to God, there will be concern about the camper's relationship to God and an opportunity for evangelism in camp.

5. Since social values are important, but not all-important, there will be an endeavor to develop these among the campers in small and larger group living situations.

6. Use may be made of the project method of instruction, problem-solving, etc. But both the director and the children will know beforehand the goals to be accomplished. The counselor is a teacher and a guide. The burden of curriculum planning will not be placed upon immature minds. The camper will be helped in self-expression, but, more important, he will be encouraged to develop self-discipline.

7. There will be definite teaching on rules of conduct for camp and for all of life.

8. The camp will have firm but kind leadership. Campers will be given a choice in certain areas and may be allowed some form of democratic control in cabins, etc. The counselors and director hold the authority, based on Biblical patterns.

EVANGELICALS MAY BE CONFIDENT

When the evangelical realizes the bases for his pattern in camping, he may be as confident in his choice as is the pragmatist in his.

For further encouragement: Since Sputnik, and since the discovery of so many Johnnys who cannot read, Susies who cannot spell, and, worse, of the moral decay of a whole generation of Americans, which many sociologists blame on the loose standards of pragmatism, this philosophy and progressive education are on the defensive. Traditionalists in education groups are daring again to lift their voices against progressive educational theories and practices.

❖❖❖❖❖❖❖❖

4. CAMPING OBJECTIVES

BLENDING CAMPER, PARENT, AND CAMP OBJECTIVES

Every camp is confronted with the task of harmonizing three separate sets of objectives—those of the parents, campers, and camps. No camp is successful unless it can blend these three. For even if the camp's objectives are achieved at the cost of the child's unhappiness or the parent's objections, attendance at future camps is jeopardized. Synchronizing these three sets of desires is the work of everyone on the camp staff. Hence every camp staff member should be made well aware of exactly what the objectives are for his camp circumstances.

Ask any early youth why he wants to go to camp and you will receive a quick and frank answer that represents his mood at the moment:

"So I can swim in the lake."

"To see the kids I met last year."

" 'Cause we go on a moonlight hike."

Children are not interested in high-sounding objectives such as "personality development" or "growth in democratic processes." A summary of the underlying motives of campers will reveal that their goal is to "have a good time" or "have fun."

The following listing of camper objectives, given by Mrs. Clara

Hester of the faculty of Indiana University at an ACA Institute, is
used by permission.

What children desire in a camping experience:
1. Above all—to have fun
2. Good food
3. Excitement—adventure
4. New experiences
5. Approval and being liked

It should be pointed out that in the context of a Christian camp
"having fun" may include religious experiences. Even as adults find
deep satisfaction in times when God's presence becomes very real
either with others or alone, so children have the same enjoyments.
Said the psalmist, "In thy presence is fulness of joy" (Ps. 16:11).
Children can experience this supreme joy in camp at the high
moments when Christ's presence becomes real, be it in the woods
examining the works of God's hand, at vespers on the lakeshore, or
alone in a place of private devotion. Some of the choicest and
longest-cherished memories of camp may be times of spiritual
awareness.

The parents have a different viewpoint. One may pass swiftly
over the working mother who nonchalantly stated that she sent her
child to camp "because it was cheaper than a baby-sitter," and
the couple who intended to go on a vacation and wanted a place
"to stow Junior awhile."

An underlying motive which probably will not be expressed by
parents or even recognized by them is the desire to conform. It is
becoming the popular thing to send one's children to camp. While
the parent may be unaware of it, the desire "to keep up with the
Jones children," who go to camp, will have a subconscious but
not major influence. The mother says, "I just think it will do him
good to go to camp." Father expresses it, "It'll toughen the kid
up to get him away from his Mom's apron strings awhile."

But to be kept in mind is the prime requisite of camping as far
as the parents are concerned—the safety of their child. They'll be
glad for anything beneficial he learns at camp, but they want him
back all in one piece.

Mrs. Hester gives these goals that parents want camps to achieve in relation to their children.

1. Safety of the child—kept from accident
2. Health guarded by proper food and rest, and cleanliness
3. Reasonable control, not harsh, dictatorial, but set limits to give the child a sense of security
4. Some skills achieved, such as being taught to swim
5. Progress in getting along with others
6. Learning of some independence (cutting of parental apron strings)
7. Fostering of neatness (which can hardly be achieved at camp without previous patterns taught at home)

A Christian parent sending his child to an evangelical camp will offer his prayers for accomplishment of another goal:

> Spiritual growth of the child, finding Christ as Saviour if he has not been born again; learning to serve Him better if the child has already been converted

Since camp objectives vary with each camp, they will be divided into three groups for further study: those of *secular camping, church camping of the more liberal type, and evangelical camping.*

OBJECTIVES IN SECULAR CAMPING

It is not difficult for secular camping authorities to agree that camping is an educational venture. It is worthwhile, then, to examine the objectives of secular education in general to discover the relationship of camping to the total educational process.

The Educational Policies Commission of the National Education Association gives four broad objectives in terms of pupils' needs, stating that the home, parents, schools, and social agencies all share in accomplishing these:[1]

Self-realization: to learn new things, improve oneself, gain health, properly direct one's life.

Human relationships: to learn social skills and appreciation of others. Peace among nations and good will between men depend

---

[1] Reuel A. Benson and Jacob A. Goldberg, *The Camp Counselor* (New York: McGraw-Hill Book Company, 1951), p. 20.

on competence in this area. Lack of knowledge of other people and their needs leads to friction.

Economic efficiency: to learn to make a living successfully, showing improvement in economic skills, managing one's life.

Civic responsibility: to find one's place in the community, to live by the laws of his society and conserve its resources, to better it.

Secular camping is making an effective effort to achieve these aims in some degree in its camping program. For example, while vocational training is not specifically taught at camp, attitudes of self-reliance, independence, and perseverance, which tie into job efficiency, are goals to be achieved at camp. State Benson and Goldberg, "The camp environment, its social setting, and its varied activities make it an ideal place for accomplishing many of our basic educational objectives." [2]

But summer camping has objectives of its own that are amplifications of those considered above. The American Camping Association gives the following objectives of camps in general, and some possible outcomes.

1. The development of a sense of "at-home-ness" in the natural world and the art of outdoor living.
   a. Increased understanding and appreciation of the world of nature.
   b. A keener sense of responsibility for the conservation of natural resources.
   c. Understanding of man's dependence on nature.
   d. Ability to use basic camping skills.
2. Education for safe and healthful living.
   a. Ability to use basic camping skills.
   b. Improved eating habits and nutritional status.
   c. Increased vitality, endurance and strength.
   d. The formation of positive health habits.
   e. Adjustment to physical defects.
   f. Safety skills indigenous to the out-of-doors.
   g. Freedom from mental tensions.
3. Education for constructive use of leisure.
   a. Ability to camp with ease.
   b. Development of a variety of skills useful in adult life.

[2] *Ibid.*, p. 21.

    c. Creative ability in developing recreational activities.

    d. Increased understanding and appreciation of the out-of-doors.

4. Contribution to personality development.

    a. Development of increased self-reliance and initiative.

    b. Adjustment to physical defects.

    c. Development of various skills.

    d. Increased creative ability.

    e. Freedom from parental control.

    f. A sense of worth as an individual through belonging to a group.

    g. Development of ability to analyze, judge, make intelligent decisions.

    h. Freedom from mental tension.

    i. An appreciation of comradeship.

    j. Ability to cooperate and be considerate of others.

    k. A sense of social understanding and responsibility.

    l. An understanding and appreciation of persons of other religions, cultures, nationalities, races.

    m. A sense of kinship with and security in an orderly universe.

5. Education for democratic group and individual living.

    a. Understanding of our pioneer heritage.

    b. A sense of worth as an individual.

    c. Development of ability to analyze, judge, make decisions.

    d. Ability to cooperate and think of others.

    e. A sense of social understanding and responsibility.

    f. Ability to function effectively in democratic society.

    g. An understanding of the worth of every individual.

6. The development of spiritual meanings and values.

    a. An understanding and appreciation for persons of other religions, cultures, nationalities and races.

    b. A deeper sense of religious values as expressed in all phases of living.

    c. A sense of kinship with and security in an orderly universe.

    d. A keener sense of aesthetic appreciation.[3]

OBJECTIVES IN GENERAL CHURCH CAMPING

General church camping, including that of a more liberal background, considers camping as a part of the Christian education program.

[3] *Camp Administration Course Outline* (Martinsville, Ind.: American Camping Association, 1961), pp. 4, 5.

After much thoughtful study by an array of eminent Christian educators, the following Christian education objectives were adopted in 1958 by the Commission on General Christian Education, National Council of the Churches of Christ in the United States of America.

The supreme purpose of Christian education is to enable persons to become aware of the seeking love of God as revealed in Jesus Christ and to respond in faith to this love in ways that will help them to grow as children of God, live in accordance with the will of God, and sustain a vital relationship to the Christian community.

To achieve this purpose Christian education, under the guidance of the Holy Spirit, endeavors:

To assist persons, at each stage of development, to realize the highest potentialities of the self as divinely created, to commit themselves to Christ, and to grow toward maturity as Christian persons;

To help persons establish and maintain Christian relationships with their families, their churches, and with other individuals and groups, taking responsible roles in society, and seeing in every human being an object of the love of God;

To aid persons in gaining a better understanding and awareness of the natural world as God's creation and accepting the responsibility for conserving its values and using them in the service of God and of mankind;

To lead persons to an increasing understanding and appreciation of the Bible, whereby they may hear and obey the Word of God; to help them appreciate and use effectively other elements in the historic Christian heritage;

To enable persons to discover and fulfill responsible roles in the Christian fellowship through faithful participation in the local and world mission of the church.[4]

There is an expectation that every type of religious program of the churches involved should make its contribution toward the fulfillment of these basics.

[4] *The Objectives in Christian Education* (New York: National Council of the Churches of Christ in the United States of America, 1958), pp. 21, 22.

Those which can best be achieved at camp are as follows:

1. To provide an experience of Christian living through which campers come to a better understanding of Christian principles and teachings, as revealed in the Bible.
2. To provide an experience of living in the out-of-doors, and to gain new knowledge of its resources, and develop skills in using them.
3. To give campers a new perspective through the experience of being away from home.
4. To help campers in their understanding of God and His purposes as they make discoveries about His work in nature.
5. To provide time for contemplation not always possible in other parts of the program of the church.
6. To let campers learn to worship God in new ways in the out-of-doors.
7. To aid campers, through small group experiences within the total camp group, to develop self reliance and responsibility as cooperative citizens of a Christian community.
8. To enable campers to have a wholesome and happy time.
9. To relate Christian growth in camp to life at home and in the church.
10. To aid in the process of developing genuine Christian fellowship based upon respect for individual worth.[5]

OBJECTIVES IN EVANGELICAL CAMPING

The over-all aim in Christian education has been given concisely by the evangelical leader James DeForest Murch: "Fitting man to live in harmony with the perfect will of God." [6]

Dr. Harold C. Mason offers a more expanded definition of the aims of Christian education in evangelical circles: "Provide learning experiences which will lead to Christian experience of Christ as Saviour and Lord. Promote the growth of Christian character, Christian living, Christian culture, and effectiveness in Christian service." [7]

[5] *Toward Better Church Camping* (Chicago: Special Committee on Camps and Conferences, International Council of Religious Education, 1950), p. 6.
[6] James DeForest Murch, *Christian Education and the Local Church* (Cincinnati: Standard Publishing Foundation, 1958), pp. 22, 23.
[7] Harold C. Mason, *Teaching Task of the Local Church* (Winona Lake, Ind.: Light and Life Press, 1960), p. 16.

Besides these, evangelicals can accept the expanded Christian education goals given by the National Council of Churches in preceding pages. These, however, because of the necessity of pleasing many groups, cannot be stated as strongly as evangelicals would desire. Hence, to them should be added Dr. Mason's aims.

As in secular and general church camping, evangelicals find camping an unexcelled opportunity for accomplishing some of the goals of evangelical Christian education. The National Education Association makes it clear that schools alone cannot achieve its goals but need the cooperation of home, parents, and social agencies. Likewise achieving objectives of evangelical Christian education requires careful functioning of each agency of the church and home. Each phase of church work contributes to the total Christian education program.

The vital contribution that camping can make to the total program of Christian education can be seen in better perspective by considering the time element. Not only is more time spent at a one-week camp than at a whole year of Sunday school, but this is consecutive and consistent time. The impact of these hours can be deep and effective.

Camping offers a unique opportunity to achieve objectives that can be accomplished better at camp than in any other part of church life. Those things which can best be accomplished in the outdoor atmosphere of camp should be done there; those that can best be achieved in the Sunday-school classroom should be done there. For example, heavy doctrinal teaching is more appropriately undertaken in the pastor's membership class than at camp.

The goals of Christian camping for evangelicals may be summarized by this listing from the Philosophy Committee of the National Sunday School Association Camp Commission.

The Christian camp should provide opportunities:

(1) to deal with campers as *individuals,* counseling them personally in the areas of their spiritual need (note Jesus' example in John 3-5);
(2) to encourage *definite spiritual decision* at the level of the camper's readiness (as in Jesus' example in John 3-5);
(3) to help establish *good habits of Christian living*—prayer, Bible read-

ing and study, personal devotions and witnessing (II Tim. 3:14-17; Acts 1:8, 2:42);

(4) to have *practical experience* in leadership, service, witnessing and application of spiritual truths to daily living (II Tim. 2:2; John 13:1-17; Luke 22:24-28; Mark 6:7).

In addition, the Christian camp seeks other outcomes related to the total development of the camper, such as:

(1) the establishment of *sound health habits*—cleanliness, adequate rest, proper diet, wholesome exercise and good attitudes toward the body as God's temple (I Cor. 6:19, 20);

(2) the profitable and wise use of *leisure time,* independent of artificial machine-made amusements (Eph. 5:15, 16);

(3) learning *outdoor skills* as a means of developing character and as training for possible future missionary work (I Cor. 9:19-27; I Cor. 10:31);

(4) development of the ability to *get along with others* unselfishly (I Cor. 13; Rom. 12:9-21);

(5) learning effective *leadership* skills (Exod. 35:30-35);

(6) learning *responsibility* for one's own decisions (Gal. 6:4-9).[8]

FROM PHILOSOPHY TO METHODOLOGY

Out of philosophy come objectives. From these then should come methodology, or the camp program. Probably many camps have been merrily staged with never a thought to the "why" (philosophy) of their camp program. The unrealized and unstated philosophy perhaps was superior to the camp program, or the converse might be true. No doubt there is much inconsistency between philosophy and methodology in all camping, both secular and religious.

Chart II is an attempt to set up methodology consistent with the philosophy and objectives that have been worked out by the authors for use in their own camps. It is not meant as a pattern for others. Each camp staff will find it beneficial to construct such a chart for its own use. No activity that does not meet one of the stated objectives should be a part of the camp program.

First, terms should be defined: *Philosophy of camping* is the basic

[8] *Guiding Principles for Christian Camping* (Chicago: National Sunday School Association, 1962), pp. 8, 9.

CHART II. PHILOSOPHY AND METHODOLOGY OF AN INDIVIDUAL CAMP

Ultimate Objective: that each camper may know Christ as Saviour and Friend

MAJOR OBJECTIVES	GENERAL OBJECTIVES	SPECIFIC OBJECTIVES	METHODS
I. Spiritual	A. Evangelism	1. That each child know Christ as Saviour	a. Evening vespers with evangelistic emphasis b. Class curriculum emphasizing plan of salvation c. Counselors watching for opening to deal personally with campers
		2. That every born-again camper learn to be a soul-winner	a. Volunteer prayer groups praying for needy campers b. Personal witnessing both public and private c. Emphasis on necessity of living consistently with testimony d. Suggesting ways of tying in evangelistic fervor of camp to home church
	B. Christian nurture (Growth in Christ)	1. Understanding principles of Christian living (indoctrination)	a. Class curriculum giving emphasis to this b. Morning chapel dealing with principles of successful Christian living c. Counselors quick to commend Christian attitudes displayed
		2. Knowing the meaning of prayer, both petition and devotion	a. Voluntary private devotions b. Voluntary prayer groups c. Public prayer at meals, chapel, classes; children participating at times d. Cabin devotions
		3. Participation in true worship	a. Appreciating God through His creation—informal worship b. Making services worshipful—communion, vesper, sunset, Galilean
		4. Sharing Christ with others through Christian testimony	a. Encouraging public testimonies b. Making witnessing and speaking about the Lord natural in daily life.

5. Sharing Christ through aroused missionary interest

   a. Missionary a staff member
   b. Letters from missionaries posted
   c. Class in study of missions
   d. Addresses of missionaries and children available for letter writing
   e. Missionary offering—special, traditional project
   f. Craft class to make items for missions

6. Teaching of stewardship

   a. Challenge campers with need for dedication of lives to God for service
   b. Tithing instruction and giving of present means
   c. Teaching that all of life belongs to God

7. Teaching of church loyalty

   a. Class in church heritage, displays from church schools, institutions
   b. New converts urged to become members of church upon return home
   c. Total atmosphere one of love and respect for standards of sponsoring church

8. Tying in camp to local church

   a. Campers encouraged to attend church regularly at home
   b. Camp echo service at local church following camp
   c. Follow-up reports to pastors on each camper

9. Scripture reading and memorization

   a. Voluntary memorization of assignments; reading, a part of devotions and services

II. Physical

A. Physical needs of camper abundantly cared for

1. Provision for adequate diet

   a. Fee sufficient for adequate menus, planned before camp
   b. Presupposes an effectively organized kitchen and dining room

CHART II (CONTINUED)

MAJOR OBJECTIVES	GENERAL OBJECTIVES	SPECIFIC OBJECTIVES	METHODS
		2. Sufficient rest	a. Abide by standards of needed rest for age group b. Expect conformity from campers c. Provide rest hour during day, longer if campers show signs of weariness
		3. Care for sickness or injury	a. Pre-camp examination by doctor b. Examination by nurse on opening day c. Camp nurse supplied with necessary medications and equipment; doctor on call d. Camp insurance for each camper
		4. Healthful exercise	a. Usually unnecessary to insist that campers get enough exercise, except in isolated cases b. More likely that some should be guarded against overexertion
		5. Provisions for safety and sanitation	a. Make every effort to meet recognized standards in waterfront, water supply, dishwashing, sanitation facilities, protection against hazards
		6. Development of health habits	a. Instruction in health habits by nurse b. Checking by counselor to encourage these
III. Social	A. To help each camper become a well-adjusted group member	1. To respect authority of leader 2. To encourage friendships	It is difficult to give exact methods for realizing these social goals. The better the counseling staff, the more of these will be attained.
		3. To learn democratic participation 4. To learn good sportsmanship	There would be a few simple rules presented in a non-autocratic way; group pressure to keep these should be encouraged by a camper's council; obedience should be expected.

5. To do his share of the work
6. To respect rights of others
7. To learn social responsibility
8. To learn independence and self-reliance
9. To insure a sense of security
10. To provide a happy, wholesome time

The youth should be given some latitude in choice of activities, encouraging his creativity. He should share in work assignments.

The cabin unit should be organized to give him security, participation in group goals, provide friends, realize that his rights are subordinate to that of the group.

IV. Educational   A. To develop new knowledge, skills, and values in various fields

1. To learn an appreciation of nature

   a. Class in nature study or informal nature study emphasis
   b. Building a nature trail
   c. Making a nature museum
   d. Nature crafts

2. To learn new recreational skills—sports and games

   a. Provide swimming instruction; lifesaving for older groups
   b. Group games
   c. Plenty of activities for free time

3. Crafts that teach

   a. Use creative crafts with natural materials as much as possible
   b. If pure crafts are taught make them as creative as possible (not pre-cut kits)

4. Leadership training

   a. Give each camper leadership position at some time in cabin or council
   b. Counselor-in-training program for older, promising campers

5. Provide for other special interests

   a. Instruction in other secular subjects: first aid, home nursing. camp newspaper, chorus, etc.

concept concerning the primary values of life that are related to camping. *The ultimate objective* is a concise statement of the camp's supreme purpose. *Major objectives* (goals or aims) are here considered the basic classification of camp purposes. These come directly from one's philosophy. *General objectives* are the simplest statements of these purposes. *Specific objectives* are the amplifications or breakdown of the general objectives. *Methods* are the avenues of accomplishing these aims. *Techniques* are the instruments of methods.

Methods and techniques compose the program of the camp. Methods will be given in a later section of this volume, but specific techniques are too detailed for this survey course and thus are not included in Chart II.

The pattern of Chart II, was formulated by Dr. M. F. Henkel and used in his class in philosophy of camping at Winona Lake School of Theology, Winona Lake, Indiana. An further use of it should give credit to him.

Only four major objectives are included. These correspond to the divisions found in Luke 2:52, "And Jesus increased in wisdom and stature and in favor with God and man." It is held unnecessary to include such categories as "moral," "emotional," or "psychological," as are given in some listings of camp objectives. With religious and social adjustment, these other matters should be taken care of.

While there is a division of religious aims from others in the chart, this does not mean that religion in camp is in a department all by itself. Rather, the religious aims should permeate all of the camp program. They are not to be realized alone in formal class periods on Bible study or during chapel service but are to be worked out as living truths in the everyday occurrences of camp. It needs to be made clear to counselors and campers that no activity in camp is purely secular. Precepts of Christian living and conduct can be shown on the ball field, during K.P. assignments, even at "lights out" time at night. Camp offers a priceless opportunity to show that Christ can be in every phase of living.

When we speak of the integration of the spiritual and secular, we are not referring to a blend of the two elements, but rather an application of the spiritual to every area of life. Hallowed by recognition of the Creator of all good, archery and horsemanship, campcrafts and swimming, and all other camp activities, are no longer secular. They are being enjoyed by Christians; Christian attitudes are employed in their use; spiritual principles are being lived through them . . . and through these activities Christ is attractively presented in a practical way.[9]

BIBLIOGRAPHY

The following books for further study in the field of camp philosophy and objectives are arranged in recommended order of purchase for the average evangelical camp. See bibliographies listed in Appendix for further related publications.

Camp Commission, National Sunday School Association. *Guiding Principles for Christian Camping.* Chicago: The Association, 1962. 50¢. (Evangelical in emphasis.)

Webb, Kenneth B. (editor). *Light from a Thousand Campfires.* New York: Association Press, 1960. $4.95.

Doty, Richard S. *The Character Dimension of Camping.* New York: Association Press, 1960. $4.75.

Division of Christian Education. *The Objectives in Christian Education.* New York: National Council of the Churches of Christ in the United States of America, 1958. 60¢.

Anyone interested in a study of the various schools of philosophy will find in the following text, available in public libraries, a detailed comparison of naturalism, idealism, realism, and pragmatism:

J. Donald Butler. *Four Philosophies and Their Practice in Education and Religion.* New York: Harper & Row, 1957. $6.00.

STUDY HELPS

1. What are the basic philosophic concepts of pragmatism?
2. What are the basic philosophic concepts of an evangelical?
3. Compare a pragmatic camp with an evangelical camp.

[9] *Why Are We Camping?* Report of the Committee on Christian Camping Philosophy (Chicago: National Sunday School Association, 1960), p. 17.

5. What are objectives in public education? In what way does camping help achieve these?
6. What are the major objectives in secular camping?
7. Do you disagree with any of the objectives in Christian education as given by the National Council of the Churches of Christ? If so, give your revisions.
8. How do objectives of general church camping fall short of the evangelical position?
9. Give two brief definitions of evangelical objectives in Christian education.
10. What are the relationships of philosophy, objectives, and methods in camping?
11. How may spiritual aims permeate the whole program in evangelical camping?

PROJECT

1. List objectives for an evangelical camp which agree with your camp philosophy.

III. WHEN TO DO WHAT

ADMINISTRATION

"To everything there is a season, and a time to every purpose under heaven."   *Ecclesiastes 3:1*

Accomplishing "great things" is made up of doing many small things at the right time and in the right way.

The first two parts of this book have presented three viewpoints in camping, endeavoring to differentiate between evangelical camping, secular camping, and general church camping with a liberal trend. The remainder of the book will give specific instruction in the mechanics of evangelical camping only, specifically short-term, resident camping for junior and junior high ages, though much that is presented will be applicable to other camping situations.

5. EVANGELICAL CAMPING NEEDS MORE PRE-PLANNING

Dr. H. C. Mason, former college president and long-time professor in Christian education in evangelical theological seminaries, is prone to tell his students, "Evangelicals are likely to just 'haul off and do things.'" This inclination to get in and see the job done even without proper training and using makeshift facilities stems from the desire to evangelize the world now—and is a commendable one! Yet a more effective job may be done if the evangelical would stop long enough to use the aids that are available to him.

The authors recall the first camp which they "hauled off" and directed nearly two decades ago. A farm truck was borrowed from one of their church members and loaded with an assortment of grocery staples, farm food, bedrolls, craft materials, and sun-tanned farm youth. The boys were joined by others from three nearby churches at the camp site—an abandoned CCC camp in the rugged eastern Cascades, at the fork where two rushing mountain streams meet. What the camp lacked in facilities it made up in scenery, untarnished naturalness, and wildlife. Wild deer roamed the clearing at dusk, and a rattlesnake was killed each day! What the staff lacked in camping finesse was at least partly compensated for by their zeal and genuine love for youth. None had seen a book on camping or heard of the ACA. But after two weeks of living first with boys, then girls, all went home convinced that they had conducted "two wonderful camps."

And who would dispute this? There had been an abundance of good food, exhilarating dips in the icy stream, hikes and fishing in lakes of that high country, songs, crafts, fun—and best of all, God was there! Every camper left camp with a testimony to God's saving grace; today a young minister dates his conversion from that camp. It *was* a wonderful camp, but in this more sophisticated era better methods are indicated.

God puts no premium on ignorance, although He will bless any effort put forth for Him. He can bless in a greater way dedicated training, system, and efficiency.

The verbatim report which follows is a recent one with names and places changed. It points up certain strengths and weaknesses still found in some evangelical camping. The authors have a high regard for such camps staffs who are doing their best, often in difficult circumstances. The report is not presented in a critical spirit. In fact, this entire book is written with the hope that such camps may be helped to more effectiveness, still keeping their priceless ingredient—the zeal to see youth brought to Christ.

Verbatim Report	*Evaluative Comments by Authors*
"I was asked to help by the Committee of the Texas camp, dates June 23-29. Although I was not present on the 28th and 29th, I'll report on when I was present.	Short-term camp. Pastors leave on Saturday.
"For the last three years this camp has been going on in the eastern part of Texas. We have included both Juniors and Junior Highs, ages ranging from 8 through 14 years. Every year the camp has been very successful. This year we had 8 8-year-olds, 16 9-years, 20 10-years, 21 11-years, 15 12-years, and 9 13-years. We had a total of 103 registered. They were not all present at the above counting for that was the first night at flag lowering.	New camp, inexperienced help. No pre-camp training. Success has various measurements. Too wide an age range. Some traveled hundreds of miles.
"On Monday, June 23, we landed at camp amidst much confusion and noisy boys and girls. The reason for the confusion was that all of the help hadn't arrived yet so that we could get started. Rev. Smith was unloading his equipment in the dining hall when I showed up about 2 P.M. The Reverend said, 'Bob, how about you sitting here in the dining hall and registering for us?' I said, 'Fine!' And so we began to take names, addresses, and money. The charge was seven dollars plus their canteen fee. At the close of registering along toward the last day we had registered a total of 103 along with 27 adult workers to	Little pre-planning. Camp director arrived same day camp begins. No pre-registering. No planned first-day routine. Fee too low to provide adequate diet.

Verbatim Report

help take care of the group. The first night there was little sleep. It was similar to those 'slumberless parties' that girls have.

Good ratio of adults to campers.

"Then Tuesday morning came too soon, for no one wanted to get up including the cooks, but we were up and the camp astir. We skipped the first class in order to get more organized for we had run out of beds the night before, so chapel began early and Pastor Bob read the rules at chapel of the do's and don't's, then the camp was officially in gear with everyone educated to the schedule and the order of the day. Everyone enjoyed Mrs. Cool's beautiful Scene-O-Felt stories and her object lessons of the morning chapel hour. Then Mrs. Hicks and Mr. Abbot taught the two classes of Bible study. We enjoyed the evangelist in the evening as Rev. Hunt brought inspiring messages and taught us many new choruses. Also the choruses of Rev. Root and his accordion were enjoyed by all, especially 'The Devil is a Sly Old Fox' and 'I'm Glad to be a Christian,' and 'Clap your Hands' and so on. Beginning Tuesday evening through Thursday evening the altar was lined with youthful seekers. When one was through praying for himself, he would go get his friends or else move over to help others pray through. These young folks had good practical Christianity for it showed in their daily life that they were changed at an altar of prayer.

Pre-registering would avoid this.

Counselors do this better in cabins.

Good extra feature.

Classes too large.

Mass evangelism has value when supplemented with personal counseling.

Camps should emphasize singing of various kinds, not only choruses.

Who we hope were carefully instructed, started in devotional habits, and given nurture literature.

Tremendous values must be preserved.

"Harry said he liked it all, and during the testimonies he said he would have testified sooner but his tooth fell out!

Good to have campers express evaluation—builds morale.

"Louise said she liked the evening service.

"Norma said she liked the handcraft and recreation.

Balanced program is essential.

"Many of the boys and girls said they love Rev. and Mrs. Baker, who operated the canteen.

Workers who love children are invaluable.

Verbatim Report

"It was too bad that the preachers won the ball game over the rest of the staff and the children. Of course, they had a preacher for an umpire. The preachers led by 14 to 11 at the top half of the ninth, so we quit.

Some do not use organized sports. Poor practice to pit staff against campers.

"We left for home on Saturday afternoon so we can't tell you the facts concerning the Saturday and Sunday services."

Undesirable to have any staff (or campers) leave early.

Signed:
Pastor Bob

◈◈◈◈◈◈◈◈

6. ORGANIZING THE CAMP

THE CAMP COMMITTEE PLANS THE CAMP

SPONSORING BODY

Except for privately owned or organized camps, most evangelical camps have a larger sponsoring body. This may be a denominational unit (district, synod, local church) or a section or district of a religious agency. When camping is begun by such a group, usually the first action is to appoint a committee, which has specific responsibility for the camp organization and operation.

THE CAMP COMMITTEE (*or Board*)

Membership on the committee should be accepted by those who are alert to present-day camping purposes and practices, willing to give their time in study, planning, and promotion. The number of members, election procedure, and term of office are determined by the sponsoring body. Staggering of terms gives continuity to board membership. Usually the sponsoring body elects the committee. Where the committee does its own electing, it has been found wise to declare a member ineligible for re-election, after his term is complete, for a period of one year. This avoids a self-perpetuating board with members feeling under obligation to re-elect a current member even if another might serve better.

Private camps do not necessarily need camp committees, for the owner is able to set policies and carry them out unrestrictedly. However, a private camp that serves a large group finds it beneficial to have the counsel and varied viewpoints of committee members. Members may be selected by the owner or elected by the committee itself.

PLANNING THE CAMP

Before he begins functioning, every camp committee member should read camping literature in order to be informed and intelligent. One of the purposes of this volume is to provide a survey course in camping for camp committee members.

It is easier for a committee to elect a director, give him a free hand, and let him assume responsibility for the resultant success or failure. But the camp committee should plan the camp. The members should conduct themselves in a businesslike way, keeping minutes, receiving reports, and appointing subcommittees as desired to carry out various phases of their work. These may include Program, Counseling, Business Management, Food Service, Site, Health, etc.

Invaluable as a working aid for the camp committee in making its basic decisions, in an old camp or a new one just beginning, is a committee workbook with guide sheets. This should be made up beforehand by the committee chairman and duplicated for each member. It should contain ten to fifteen sheets with sufficient blank space to fill in decisions as the committee makes them. A suggestive outline for such a workbook follows. This may be much more detailed, with specific questions in each area.

Camp Committee Planning Workbook

Camp Committee Organization

                                     Addresses: Phone Numbers:

     Chairman
     Secretary
     Committee Members (arranged by subcommittee assignments)
Formulating Camp Objectives (Why are we camping?)
     Spiritual   Social
     Physical   Educational
Type of Camp
     Dates: Hour of beginning: of leaving:
     Grades and sexes   first meal: last meal:
     included:
     Size of camp: No. of campers: No. of staff:
     Quota for each church:
Camp Staff
     Plans for pre-camp training
         Required reading
         Correspondence
         On-site training
     Basic qualifications of counselors
     Salaries and travel allowance
     Staff regulations
     Special training paid for by camp (Red Cross, YMCA, etc.)
Selecting Key Personnel
     Director   Business manager
     Program director   Head counselor
     Health staff
     Recruiting plans for other staff members
     Suggestive list of counselors, activity specialists, teachers, camp pastor
Camp Site
     Is it adequate for this type of camping?   New one needed?
     Contemplated improvements this year   Long range plan
     Facilities and equipment needed
     Meeting state regulations: safety, sanitation, health
Business
     Tentative budget   Setting camp fee
     Registration procedures   Health certificates required?

Insurance   Meeting legal requirements
Meeting camp standards and joining camp organizations
Promotion
    Schedule of publicity for year
    Raising finances by contribution (if necessary)
Program
    Bible curriculum   Worship activities
    Tentative schedule   Other program elements
Follow-Up and Camp Evaluation Programs
Further Committee Meetings This Year

THE CAMP DIRECTOR

When the camp committee has made basic decisions, the camp director is the one responsible for putting these into action. The success or failure of the camp will hinge largely on the consecration, ability, and personality of the camp director. Across the continent talented, able men and women are being raised up as God gives them the vision for this work. Theirs is a difficult task, but the rewards are tremendously satisfying.

The American Camping Association standards require that a camp director must have had at least "two years of experience in organized camping, experience in group leadership or educational or administrative experience in a comparable related field, should be 25 years of age or older, a graduate of a college or university or equivalent educational background."

Gunnar Hoglund gives these qualifications of a Christian camp director:

1. A good camp director is an emotionally mature adult. He does not allow tantrums, moods and whims to interfere with the daily business of solving problems.

2. He is confident of the future. Instead of complaining how difficult it is to reach the young for Christ, he plunges cheerily into his task. This optimistic spirit lasts and lasts, from one end of the week to the other.

3. He makes decisions easily. He may base them on details, but is never too close to the trees to see the forest. He likes responsibility and is not afraid to take the rap for his own errors.

4. He leads his campers. First, he wins their liking and respect, then guides and stimulates them in carrying out objectives of soul winning and

spiritual living. Yet his young people say: "With him I can always offer my two cents without having my head chopped off."

5. He has good judgment. He gets the facts, prays over them, then makes objective decisions. He doesn't blow hot all day over some idea and then forget it for a new one the next day.

6. He is adaptable. He can listen and make changes. He can "trim his sails" to work in all kinds of "weather" with all sorts of people.

7. He knows where he is going and has a strong drive to get there. He is loyal to his camp board, his pastor, and his co-workers. He has plenty of energy and staying power.

8. He is a good planner. He gets the ideas, then has others carry them out. He foresees difficulties and takes steps to avoid them.

9. He has a sense of humor. He not only shows tolerance for the weaknesses of others, but has the ability to laugh at himself when in the wrong. In brief, he's no stuffed shirt.

10. He is spiritually minded. He knows the joy of a close walk with the Lord and considers his highest reward to see his campers become rightly related to Christ.[1]

The following job description of a camp director is an excellent one:

Works with camp committee in selecting staff members. Co-operates with denominational state or area office in promoting camp. Develops registration procedure with camp committee or others involved. Is responsible for correspondence with campers, parents, and churches before camp. Plans with the camp committee and conducts precamp training of staff members, including reading, actual experience, and other learning opportunities. Directs the camp program, co-operating with entire staff and campers in its democratic developments. Keeps alert to needs, problems, ideas and possibilities within the total camp. Is the clearing house for contributions from various groups. He sets, along with his staff, the spiritual tone and tempo of camp. Counsels with staff members about program, personal concerns, in-service training, and other needs. Works with each staff member, encouraging him to carry out his responsibilities on his own teamwork with others.

The director is a counselor of counselors and becomes a counselor to campers only when aid is solicited by the counselor. Assumes final re-

[1] Gunnar Hoglund, *How to Be a Camp Director or Dean* (Chicago: Baptist General Conference of America, n.d.), p. 11.

sponsibility for total camp activities. Arranges for resource persons, events, etc., in camp. Makes all necessary arrangements and agreements with camp management. Presides over staff meetings. Checks on details of operation throughout the camp, so that the way is clear for successful achievement of goals. Keeps records himself, and gathers records from staff in order to make a valuable report to the camp committee and the denominational headquarters. Directs the evaluation of every phase of the camp and compiles this information so it can be used by future camp leaders.[2]

This further private word to camp directors should be added: Camp does not exist for the purpose of building up the ego of the camp director. It is not necessary that he should be in the limelight at every public gathering—leading the flag raising, being in charge at mealtimes, leading the singing and presiding over each service. There are others who can and should do some of these things. The camp is a better one if the camp director realizes that part of his responsibility is to train others to be able to take over his job. Next year (who knows?) the present camp director may be elsewhere.

Some camps have been greatly weakened by the camp director's assuming too much responsibility, not allowing others to have authority in their areas. This results in lack of cooperation and the camp becomes a "one-man affair." The wise camp director will stay in the background as much as possible. A bit of Oriental verse makes this point clearly:

> A leader is *best*
> When people hardly know he exists
> Not so good when people acclaim him
> Worse when they despise him.
> Fail to honor people
> They fail to honor you.
> But of a good leader who talks little,
> When his work is done, his aim fulfilled,
> They will all say,
> "We did this ourselves."
>
> —Lao-tse

[2] *Church Camping for Junior Highs* (Philadelphia: Westminster Press, 1960), pp. 43, 44.

CAMP ORGANIZATIONAL STRUCTURE

In providing for an efficient camp one of the most important steps is to establish a "chain of command." To avoid frustrations and poor interpersonal relationships, each staff member must know to whom he is directly responsible. Too, the superior staff member must be willing to delegate authority and, having done so, leave it that way. He must not bypass his assistant to make decisions that are properly made by the latter, or interfere in situations that should be handled at a lower level. In difficult situations, of course, the assistant may always—and should—seek the advice of his superior.

There is no "correct" camp organizational chart. This must be tailor-made according to the objectives, program, duration, size, and facilities of the individual camp. The following examples illustrate camps with different programs.

CHART III.

SPONSORING AGENCY
|
CAMP COMMITTEE
|
DIRECTOR
|

HEALTH	FOOD	PROGRAM	MAINTENANCE	BUSINESS
Doctor	Dietician	Head Counselor	Caretaker	Manager
Nurse	Kitchen	Activity and	Helpers	Assistant
First Aid	Dining Room	Unit Leaders		Clerical
		Counselors		
		Specialists		

Chart III shows organizational structure for a camp[3] that is obviously large and owns its own camp site; it probably has a year-round or all-summer-long program. Camping is probably decentralized, with the counselors doing any instructional work.

[3] *Camp Administration Course Outline* (Martinsville, Ind.: American Camping Association, 1961), p. 6.

CHART IV
CAMP ORGANIZATIONAL CHART

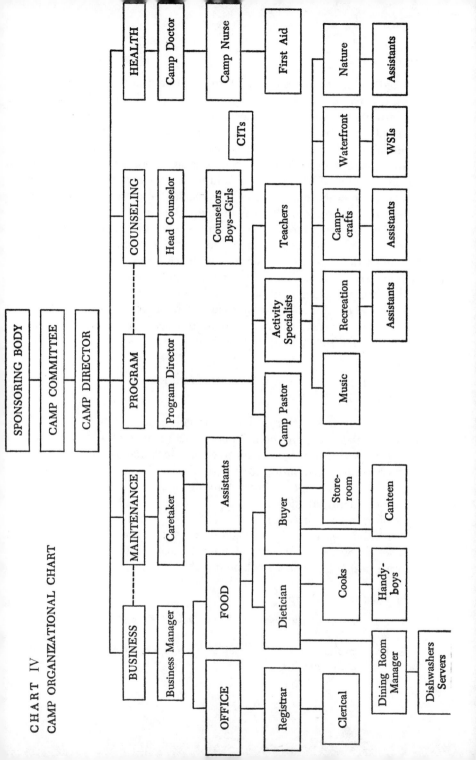

Chart IV fits the camping pattern of the authors, revealing their bias. It is based on the conviction that teachers of Bible classes need not always be counselors, counselors need not always be teachers, and both may be assistants to the activity specialists. Between program and counseling there is a close tie. Between business and maintenance there is also close cooperation. The business manager is given direction of both the office and food services and in some cases may also supervise maintenance. Five persons at most are responsible directly to the director. This is usable in year-around or short-term camping. Larger camps will have separate persons for most of these positions. In smaller camps one person will assume several duties.

Camps that operate all summer with one-week camping periods will have some designated as permanent staff, usually administrative and activity personnel. Program staff and counselors may change week by week. It is a good plan to ask such temporary staff members to serve two weeks, staggering their terms so that each week no more than half of the staff will be new.

CALENDAR FOR CAMP COMMITTEE AND DIRECTOR

The ability to get things done is largely a matter of timing and effective scheduling. Without a plan of action, a camp director after a session with his camp committee may feel that he needs to do as Stephen Leacock stated in "Gertrude the Governess," "He flung himself from the room, flung himself upon his horse and rode madly off in all directions." But a pattern of "when to do what" will give purpose and direction.

The following calendar is suggestive only. It includes items that are not necessary in all types of camps. Each camp may use it as a pattern in making its own calendar.

First Month After Camp

1. Complete the tasks listed in "Last Day at Camp," Part VI of this volume.

2. From evaluation sheets of all staff, compile recommendations to present to camp committee.

3. Receive inventory of supplies from each department head with his recommendations as to future purchases.

4. Send letter to parents, reporting camp highlights.

5. Send to participating pastors and churches follow-up reports on their campers.

6. Evaluate work of each staff member, writing appreciation letters to each, and requesting satisfactory ones to return.

7. Send report of camp to sponsoring body, or denominational headquarters.

8. Pay all bills and send in insurance report.

9. End fiscal year; have books audited.

10. Begin articles of what happened in camp in periodicals of sponsoring body.

September

1. Schedule first full committee meeting.

2. Set camp date, ages for each session, and camp fee.

3. Appoint camp director for next season.

4. Appoint key personnel as far as possible.

5. Consider evaluations and recommendations from last year's staff.

6. Carefully consider each question in the Camp Committee Planning Workbook as presented in this chapter.

7. Plan a campers' reunion for fall.

8. Plan a camp newssheet for periodic distribution to mailing list.

9. Pinpoint responsibility for next season—promotion and publicity, printing, films; recruiting of staff, site selection; maintenance; program; finance, etc.

10. Order books on camping for study by staff and committee.

October

1. Committee and director plan to attend NSSA camp workshops and CCA fall convention scheduled this month.

2. Start staff recruiting program; begin with pastors, urging them to give at least one week.

3. See that camp is prepared for winter, if climate makes this necessary.

4. Plan camping workshops in church conventions. Urge churches to schedule leadership and training courses in camping, in their regular training sessions or unions.

5. If site is rented, complete arrangements for rental next season.

November

1. Send pastors information on dates, ages, fee for next camp.
2. Program director and director select curriculum and theme for camp.
3. Send mailing explaining how parents, grandparents, or friends may give camperships for next season to their favorite campers as Christmas gifts.

December

1. Send a Christmas letter to last year's campers or prospects. In snow areas this may include a snow scene of camp site.
2. Make first arrangements for securing surplus food.
3. Employ cooks.

January

1. Renew membership in ACA and CCA.
2. Continue recruiting.
3. Print and mail first promotional flyer, posters for bulletin board.
4. Keep camp film scheduled from now through May.
5. Distribute camp stamp books.
6. Urge churches to offer camperships to worthy youth.
7. Schedule second committee meeting to approve budget; study ACA camp standards, requesting visitation if not yet approved; plan pre-camp training sessions; have report of program director on tentative plans.
8. Urge prayer support of camp throughout spring and during camp season by local churches.
9. Staff recruiting should be completed.

February

1. Order curriculum and resource materials and distribute to staff.
2. Urge all personnel to read camping literature between now and camp, to enroll in training sessions provided by Red Cross, ACA, etc.
3. Begin registration period, distributing forms to cooperating churches. Do not limit this to pastors, but also send promotional materials to Sunday-school superintendents, teachers, and other leaders of camp ages.
4. Business manager meets with cooks to work out menus and food list.
5. Plan to attend ACA conventions usually scheduled this month or in March.

March

1. Make application for insurance.
2. Begin spring preparation of camp site.
3. Request a camp library from public library.
4. Attend CCA regional convention scheduled this month or next.

April

1. Schedule an in-camp training session for all camp staff.
2. Schedule a Camper's Visit to camp site.
3. As soon as registration is received, send each pre-registrant a welcoming letter, receipt for pre-registration fee, and physical examination form.
4. Assign specific groups to counselors.
5. Check with activities specialist concerning affiliating with National Rifle Association, Camp Archery Association, etc.
6. Attend NAE Convention camping workshop, if in your area.

May

1. Complete camp site preparation; cooperate in work days.
2. Re-examine all legal aspects of camp for any change in regulations, obtaining camp license, if required in your state.
3. Check health and safety factors in camp, having drinking and swimming water checked.
4. Attend ACA training institute for your section, usually in each state.
5. Urge local churches to intensify camp promotion, giving recognition to campers planning to attend.
6. Schedule another camp committee meeting for final review of plans and policies.

Last Month Before Camp

1. Close registration, obtaining all pre-registration forms.
2. See that all camp staff have health examinations as required by law.
3. Give camp site last-minute safety inspection. May camp insect control be improved, etc.?
4. See that nurse has made arrangements for physician to be on call and that she has "standing orders" from him.
5. Send campers final letter with instructions necessary.

DECIDING CAMP SIZE, SEXES, AGES, DATE, DURATION, FEE

SIZE OF CAMP

Some camp authorities advise that no camp for early youth exceed sixty in enrollment for most satisfactory results. Others state that an enrollment of one hundred is the maximum for an efficient camp. Actually the limit of effectiveness in a camp depends upon camp philosophy, camp facilities, site, and staff. These observations regarding camp enrollment are pertinent:

1. A camp that registers over one hundred must usually be more regimented in its procedures. The rule is, the larger the camp, the less freedom for the individual, unless the camp is divided into units or sub-camps. A more relaxed atmosphere exists in smaller camps, with campers and staff given more opportunity to become closer in spirit.

2. Many expenses of a camp decrease in proportion to increase in enrollment. Estimates indicate that the camp of most economical size is one with an enrollment of 120.

3. When a camp reaches its maximum capacity, it should divide. This may be done by (a) division into separate weeks for junior and junior high ages (this should be encouraged, as they have much more successful camps separately); (b) expansion of camp facilities to care for sub-camps; (c) division of the patron territory into areas or districts, the churches from one area having their camp at the central site one period; those from another, the next period; (d) beginning new camps in other areas, especially in conferences or divisions covering large territories; (e) division of the camp by sex.

COEDUCATION?

The question of coeducational camping vs. separate camping is sure to bring a lively discussion in any camping workshop. Proponents of separate camping point out the following:

1. Boy-girl problems are eliminated. These appear particularly in junior high camps, for girls are usually more aggressive than boys at this age level.

2. A more relaxed atmosphere results, with more opportunities for serious decisions.

3. There are privileges in programming not possible with both sexes present.

Those who favor coeducational camping state these opinions:

1. Churches should not seek to avoid boy-girl problems but should teach youth how to cope with them.

2. Camps should be held within the framework of normal human relations, not divorced from reality—a criticism too often made of camps.

3. Camping is an educational experience. Public education long ago adopted coeducation as a basic tenet.

4. An only child, or a child from a home where children are of one sex, needs the opportunity to live informally with peers of the other sex.

5. "Crushes" on either men or women staff members are avoided more easily when junior high girls are with boys in camp.

6. When husband and wife teams are permitted, counselor recruiting is eased.

7. Coeducational camp directors usually see the advantage of having certain camp activities divided by sex.

Successful camps have been held and will continue to be held using either pattern. Most church camping is coeducational; private religious camps and agency camps are more likely to have separate groups.

AGES IN CAMP

Junior high camps enroll those who are in grades seven through nine. Some camps enroll youngsters who have completed these grades; others prefer to enroll those who are entering these grades in the fall. The latter system is more satisfactory to the campers, who are promoted by public schools in June and resent still being classed (for example) as "sixth-graders" when they already consider themselves "seventh-graders." Junior age camps include those who are in grades four, five, and six, with the same plan in allowing them to enroll. Problems are avoided when camps are divided by grade rather than age, and level of achievement will be more uniform.

It is a firm opinion of the authors that junior and junior high sections should be kept separate in camp. There are always more juniors, who are more responsive. Too frequently they will "run off with" the camp if left with the older age groups. If it is necessary to have them on the same camp site, provide separate chapels and keep all activities as separate as possible.

SETTING CAMP DATES

No rule can be laid down here that will apply to all camps. Consideration should be given to other meetings of the church groups, crops which youth help to harvest, and conflict with Daily Vacation Bible School programs at home churches. If family outings are planned for Fourth of July or other holidays, camp attendance is often cut during that week, a factor to be considered especially by churches scheduling only one camp period during the summer.

HOW MANY DAYS IN CAMP?

Studies show that the average short-term camp is seven days. Some denominations urge their camp committee to schedule no camp less than a week, since camp increases its benefits every day it is held over seven. In any camp for early youth it takes from three to five days for campers to "settle down," and for barriers between campers and counselors to break down. Thus a camp less than a week long ends just about the time it is really beginning to function smoothly. Many secular camps will accept no registrations for less than four weeks, feeling that they cannot accomplish their objectives in less time. The church camp, especially if the church works with its youth in midweek activities all year—with camp an extension of that program—does not need long-term camping as do private camps lacking any other contact with their youth. But many church groups are seeing the advantage of adding more days to their camping time.

It is true that extra days added to short-term camping increase its value. An immense amount of basic work and planning goes into every camp whether it is held for three days or two weeks. For the best possible returns on this investment, the camp should be held as long as possible—never for less than six or preferably seven days for early youth.

Camps can successfully begin any day of the week. Saturday is favored because that is the day parents can most easily bring children to camp. Monday is popular in religious camps, because Sunday comes as a climax and day of relaxation before going home. Many camps that must rely on pastors to carry the burden begin on Monday and close on Saturday, enabling the minister to be in his pulpit on Sunday morning. Perhaps if churches understood the benefit to the campers in this extra day of camping, they would favor their pastors' remaining at camp over Sunday.

SETTING THE CAMP FEE

So many variable factors enter into church camping that fees range from approximately one to three or four dollars a day. The cost of camp and the resulting fee will depend on (1) whether the site is purchased and maintained largely through the fees or whether this cost is borne by the sponsoring body; (2) the number of paid staff members; (3) the number and size of contributions; (4) donations of food by the sponsoring church or individuals (canning bees for camp are popular in some areas; less frequent but appreciated is the donation of a whole beef by an interested farmer).

The fee should be comparable to that charged by other church or agency camps of the area. The food budget should not be slighted in order to set a lower fee.

PUBLIC RELATIONS, PROMOTION,
AND PUBLICITY

Each camp needs to create a favorable "public image." It must let its own particular public know of its purposes and program and, in evangelical camping, obtain prayer support. There are three objectives of public relations in camping: to interpret camping to its constituency, to recruit campers and staff, and to aid in financing the camp if it is not subsidized.

The following are possible channels of interpretation:

PERSON TO PERSON

1. Camp reunions. Schedule these for fall or spring on the camp site, inviting all former or prospective campers and their families. Favorite camp activities and traditions are highlighted, building camp morale.

2. Conventions or other meetings. The camp director should welcome and even seek opportunities to present his camp at conventions or other gatherings in interpretative addresses, showing the camp film, or conducting workshops.

3. Guests at the camp site. Seeing a camp in action has sold many such visitors on the value of camping. Adequate safeguards should be set up to keep visiting from disrupting camp program. Visitor's Day can be a scheduled part of camp with regulations known to both guests and campers.

PRINTED MATERIALS

1. Camp folder. This should be as attractive as the camp budget can allow. It is sent out to all on the camp mailing list and to cooperating pastors and youth directors. It should include:

Name and date of camp on the first page.

Camp purpose stated briefly and appealingly.

Camp mail address and camp location with clear directions for finding the camp site.

Cost of tuition, and a statement concerning extra spending money and indicating whether money for crafts, insurance, etc., is included or extra.

Features of the program.

Age of campers included.

Hours of opening and closing of camp and when first and last meals are served.

Principal staff members and sponsoring body.

Pictures of camp activities or staff to add to appearance of folder.

A list of things to bring. (Be specific. If certain apparel is banned, say so. Some folders suggest that parents put name tags in clothing and list articles sent. Some state that camp will not be liable for accidents above any that are covered by insurance.)

Sometimes camps prefer to give some of this information in the letter that goes to campers after their pre-registration is received. An effective advertising method is to print a series of folders, each beamed to its audience. One, stressing speaker, goes to pastors; one, emphasizing health and safety features, to parents; and one, highlighting program features, to campers.

2. Posters for church bulletin boards.

3. Camp newssheet. In agency and private religious camping that does not have what is considered the "captive campers" of the denominational camps, it is valuable to have a newssheet as a through-the-year contact. This keeps or arouses interest of former and future campers and prospective contributors.

4. Direct mail. A Christmas letter, the new camp folder, and promotional letters are valuable, sent to the whole camp mailing list.

5. Picture post cards of camp. Use for direct mail releases and for sale in camp store.

6. Sweatshirts, tee shirts, hats, and novelties printed with the camp insignia. These serve a double purpose of advertising and profit.

MASS MEDIA

1. Articles in conference papers, denominational periodicals. Human interest or interpretative stories may well feature camping.

2. Newspaper releases. These may be prepared before camp for release to home-town papers, giving names of campers from that locale in the last paragraph. Any special camping event should merit newspaper publicity.

3. Radio and television. Announcements of camp may be woven into existing religious broadcasts. Spot announcement time may be purchased profitably in some situations. Studios near the camp are often willing to arrange special interviews with campers and staff.

VISUALS

1. Displays. At conventions or county fairs a display from an individual camp gives good publicity.

2. Movies and slides of the camp. These do one of the most effective selling jobs when imaginatively edited and when pho-

tography is good. *Caution:* use only quality photography. Be ruthless in discarding too dark, too light, or poorly composed pictures.

3. Photographs. Use in displays, in camp publicity, in articles to add veracity and interest.

PUBLICITY IN LOCAL CHURCHES

1. Snapshots of camp. Displayed on the church bulletin board, these help advertise the camp. Camp posters and folders should be on the board from January until camp season.

2. References to camp. Frequent reference to camp at youth services should encourage early youth to attend.

3. The church bulletin.

4. Sunday-school assembly period. An opportunity to advertise camp through a skit or otherwise, presented before the proper departments, may be requested.

5. Calls. To obtain final permission and to give parents definite information as to details, visits to homes are most helpful. A telephone call made personally to each youth about attending is the least that should be done.

6. Notice in the local paper. A listing of those who are to attend camp, and a résumé of interesting features, should be placed in the local paper.

7. Poster contest. Displaying the best entries submitted in a camp poster contest in succeeding weeks on the church bulletin board adds interest.

8. Camperships. Often older people whose children are grown will, if properly challenged, gladly provide funds for a child's camp tuition. Churches themselves may well invest some of their funds in providing camperships as awards for achievements, or in underwriting the fee for needy children.

9. Camper evaluation. As soon as camp season is over, campers should appear in the local church services, giving their impression of camp, particularly their testimonies as to spiritual victories won.

STAMPS FOR CAMPS

Many camps provide stamps similar to trading stamps to help youth save for or earn their way to camp. Stamps and books are supplied by the camp or denominational headquarters at small cost to churches. Stamps of one color are purchased by the children to be pasted in the books as they bring their money during the year. This money is kept by the treasurer of the groups using the stamp plan. Stamp books are transferable and redeemable, or they may be held over until the next year.

Stamps of another color are given as awards for various achievements in the local church, e.g., for perfect Sunday-school attendance, memory work, bringing others, awards in essay, poster, temperance contests, etc.

LEGAL ASPECTS OF CAMPING

Government regulations that affect camping are becoming more numerous. These must be observed. The camp director or business manager is charged with the responsibility of being informed on the following federal, state, or local regulations that are applicable in his locale and to his type of camping:

Licensing of camp by state board of health, public welfare, or recreation.

Meeting all health and safety requirements such as those pertaining to medical examination of food handlers and other staff members, housing, water and milk supply, sewage and garbage disposal, waterfront, fire prevention.

Social security tax on salaried employees.

Unemployment compensation, if necessary.

Licensing of camp store.

Collecting sales tax, if required.

Workmen's compensation laws.

Regulations on bus owned by camp.

Minimum wage law with all volunteers signing proper releases.

Fishing regulation.

Boating laws.

Use of public lands, if desired.

Building codes, if construction is done.

Surplus food commodities and other government surplus.

In Canada: government subsidy for camps of specified duration.

MEETING STANDARDS OF
NATIONAL ORGANIZATIONS

AMERICAN CAMPING ASSOCIATION

The American Camping Association is the authoritative voice of organized camping in America. In Canada the Canadian Camping Association occupies a similar position. (See addresses in Appendix.) The influence of these groups in giving camping morale and professional attitudes has been invaluable. The ACA developed from a sequence of events:

1903 One hundred camp personalities met in Boston to plan cooperatively.
1910 Camp Directors Association of America founded.
1916 National Association of Directors of Girls Camps formed.
1921 Midwest Camp Directors Association organized.
1935 Combined to form the American Camping Association.

In 1962 the ACA had forty-two sections in seven regions. National conventions are held every two years, with regional conventions in alternate years. The official organ, *Camping Magazine,* is included with membership, which is open to individuals and camps that can qualify.

Standards of the American Camping Association should be studied carefully by every camp committee and staff member and used as a guide to improved camping. The standards apply to these areas: Personnel; Program; Camp Sites, Facilities, and Equipment; Administration; Health; Sanitation; Safety and Transportation. Order *ACA Camp Standards,* 10¢ each from ACA Headquarters.

Increasingly, evangelical camps are receiving ACA membership seals, denoting their having reached a certain standard of excellence. While the standards are high, attaining them should be the goal of every evangelical camp. There is no excuse for some conditions that are tolerated in some church camps. For membership in ACA, application must be made to the local section. One of the Association's visitors will inspect the camp. If it complies with a certain percentage of ACA standards, membership is granted and use of the ACA membership seal approved. Camps not approved during the first visitation may have provisional membership until they do comply, with a three-year limitation. Very valuable to any camp anticipating visitation is the report form used by visitors: *Standards, Report of Camping Practices for Resident Camps*, 20¢ each.

STANDARDS OF OTHER GROUPS

Individual denominations and youth groups have set standards for their member camps. Each camp should be familiar with those of its sponsoring body or the organization with which it is affiliated, and should strive to meet them. A copy of the standards may be obtained from denominational or organizational headquarters.

BENEFITS FROM INTER-CHURCH CAMPING ORGANIZATIONS

The *Camp Commission of the National Sunday School Association*, an affiliate of the National Association of Evangelicals, is the coordinating group on the highest executive level in evangelical camping. The Commission has in the early 1960's perfected a stronger organization and is offering increasing assistance to camps. Its membership is invitational, limited to only one representative from a denomination or youth movement. It sponsors workshops open to the public in the fall NSSA and in spring NAE conventions. State- and regional-level NSSA conventions are also scheduling camping workshops which merit attendance of camp staff and committee members. Camping literature is available from the NSSA Camp Commission. (See address in Appendix.)

The *Christian Camp and Conference Association* (CCA) is a union of some previous evangelical camping groups. Its work is on the grass-roots level. Individuals as well as camps may become members of this organization and share in its benefits. It has several publications, notably the magazine *Christian Camps and Conferences* (included with membership), which offer inspiration and technical assistance to camping personnel. Workshops and conventions are scheduled in various areas of the nation, open to all. (See address in Appendix.)

The *National Council of the Churches of Christ* in the United States of America has a *Division on Camps and Conferences*. Its publications are of value in church camping. (See address in Appendix.)

FOLLOW-UP

There is a danger that camp may become a dream world, divorced from the reality of the camper's everyday life at home. The closing of camp too often seems like the end of a chapter, with little correlation with events that follow.

Efforts must be made at camp to counteract this tendency. The camper should be given instruction on carrying home the spiritual benefits of camp. He is to be encouraged to be loyal to the church, to counsel with pastor or youth director about problems as they arise, to witness to unsaved friends and relatives. Suitable devotional books should be recommended. Most of all, a plan of daily Bible reading and prayer should be outlined.

To help the church in its follow-up program a report of the camper's spiritual progress at camp should be sent to the pastor immediately at close of camp. Some pastors, perhaps, will do nothing with it, but many will. The home church should capitalize on returning campers' spiritual gains by giving time for testimonies in services. Some churches make it a habit to receive junior members the Sunday after their campers return.

While camper reunions and newssheets (used most often in camps without denominational sponsorship) are regarded as promotional devices, they certainly may also be considered within the framework of spiritual nurture of camp converts. They need to be planned with this aspect in mind.

Campers who return to homes that are unchurched or areas where there is no evangelical witness merit special attention. They should be provided with devotional material by the camp itself.

Recommended is the Youth for Christ follow-up correspondence course for converts, at primary, junior, and teen-age levels. For each level there are tracts to be given out at decision time, and at stated times following it; a follow-up course with worksheets to be returned to the mailer are also provided, to be mailed out each week for four to six weeks.

Junior Decision Tracts: 3 titles, 3¢ each, $1.50 per 100
Hidden Treasure Course, 4 lessons, 8¢ per set, 6¢ per set in lots of 100 or
more
Teen Decision and nurture tracts: 4 titles, 3¢ each, $1.50 per 100
Treasures Unlimited Course, 6 lessons, 10¢ per set, 8¢ in lots of 100
Order from Youth for Christ, Wheaton, Illinois 60187

The authors have prepared a nurture pamphlet for early youth: *Being a Christian, A Guide to Happy Living for Early Youth* (Light and Life Press, Winona Lake Ind. 46590; single copy 15¢, 10¢ each in quantity). This may be given to each camper on closing day and is to be kept in his Bible. It is now used in various denominations and provides helpful information for young converts and a check sheet for measuring spiritual progress. *Becoming a Christian, The Beginning of a Happy Life* is a companion publication, explaining how to become a Christian (same price and publisher).

The Navigator's Course for new converts will be valuable to older campers. Materials may be ordered from The Navigators, Colorado Springs, Colorado 80901.

The follow-up from on the succeeding page has been designed by the authors for use in evangelical camps.

CONFIDENTIAL REPORT OF COUNSELOR ON SPIRITUAL PROGRESS OF CAMPER FOR HOME CHURCH FOLLOW-UP

Name of Camper   Grade

Home Address

(Check before those which apply to this camper)

At Beginning of Camp
_____ Testified to being converted
_____ Member of sponsoring church
_____ Member of another church. Give name:
_____ Parents members of another church. Give name:
_____ Little understanding of conversion

Devotional Habits Observed
_____ Private devotions daily

_____ Read Bible by himself
_____ Memorized assigned scriptures
_____ Memorized additional scriptures
_____ Took part in cabin devotions
_____ Attended voluntary camper prayer meetings
_____ Gave public testimony

Spiritual Advancement
_____ Sought the Lord publicly for:
_____ Sought the Lord privately with help of:
_____ Apparently made little spiritual progress
_____ Made the following spiritual progress and contributed to
spiritual life of camp:

_____ Had spiritual problem concerning:

For Follow-Up Action by Home Church
_____ Indicated that he wished to become a member of the church
_____ Asked for prayer for:

Additional Comments by Counselor
Participation in total camp program: _____ excellent, _____ good,
_____ fair, _____ poor
Special needs:

Signed: _____
Counselor

Send to: Local Church _____ Pastor _____

EVALUATION

Nothing in camping method or practice is inviolate. Some phases
of camping that looked all right before the campers arrived may
have proved less than successful in practice. Hence, after camp is
over, it should be reviewed in retrospect to see what have been
its strengths and weaknesses.

Some long-term camps require the staff to stay a day after camp

closes for evaluation sessions. Short-term camps find this very difficult. Then, too, it is easier to express opinions on paper than before
the one it might concern. Evaluation sheets have proved their use-
fulness. These should be given to the staff during pre-camp training
and discussed to some extent then in order that, during the camp,
staff members may be observant (not critical). Before leaving the
camp site each staff member should turn his evaluation sheets in to
the office. They may be signed or unsigned as the director prefers.
He examines them to help in formulating recommendations to his
camp committee.

Check sheets for campers have been used to advantage in some
camps. These should not ask for written opinions, which are impossible to tabulate, but provide objective questions requiring a
check for an answer, such as:

I thought the food was _____ good, _____ average, _____ poor.
My counselor was _____ too strict, _____ about right, _____ not strict
    enough.

The evaluation sheets for counselors should provide opportunity
to give comments on every part of camp. One designed by the
authors is shown here. In actual use, ample space should be provided
for detailed comment on each phase.

CAMP EVALUATION SHEET FOR STAFF

Position of Staff Member: Period at Camp:
Previous Years on Staff: Ages Served:

To help the Camp Committee in planning future camps, please give below
thoughtful, frank, and very specific comments on each phase of the camp
program.

AREAS OF CAMPING	STRENGTHS	WEAKNESSES

Pre-Camp Training
  Home reading of required
    books
  Staff manual
  On-site training

AREAS OF CAMPING   STRENGTHS   WEAKNESSES

Program Activities
   Religious
      Chapel
      Devotions
      Evening vespers
   Bible class curriculum
   Camp newspaper
   Waterfront
   Campcraft program
   Nature
   Handcrafts
   Music

Health, Safety, Sanitation
   Regulations
   Facilities and equipment

Rules for Campers
   Campers' manuals

Staff
   Adequacy of supervision
   Relaxation and time off
   Staff regulations
   Staff meetings
   Staff relationships

Food and Menus

Dining-Room Procedures

Office

Store

Camp Atmosphere and Tempo

Achievement of Spiritual
   Objectives

7. HEALTH ORGANIZATION

To be effective, health organization in a camp needs the cooperation of everyone on the camp site.

The *camp director* is directly responsible for the health program. He delegates authority in this field to those he employs, but the final responsibility is his. He must be familiar with the standards of health and sanitation required in his state, and strive to meet the standards of the American Camping Association in these areas.

The *camp staff* should be instructed during pre-camp training concerning the health organization of camp. In states requiring them, each staff member should have a pre-camp physical examination and necessary inoculations. As many members as possible should be licensed under the first-aid program of the American Red Cross. Each should be alert to ways of improving health and sanitation practices during camp. Each should guard his own health in order to be at his best. Much tension between staff members in camp may be due to exhaustion.

The *camper* should bring with him to camp a pre-camp medical examination blank, though some camps require that the blank be returned before camp opens. This blank is filled in by parents as fully as possible and completed by a physician. The American Camping Association provides *Health Examination Forms* (for boys, for girls, for employees), 2¢ each. These are comprehensive and may make the examination more expensive than is desired. Some camps prefer to design their own forms with the assistance of the camp doctor.

On the opening day, the camper reports to the camp doctor or nurse, hands in the form, and is examined for any symptoms that may have recently developed. Instructions are given to report any injury, infection, or indisposition at once to the camp health officers.

THE CAMP DOCTOR

Every camp must engage a physician, making the arrangements before camp. If he does not stay on the camp site, he is to be on call for emergencies and gives written instructions to the camp nurse for dealing with day-to-day cases. It is very important that these "standing orders" be kept on file in the camp health office. A nurse has no right to give treatments without a doctor's orders. To do so invites malpractice suits. She must act under written directions of a doctor in each instance. *Suggested Policies and Standing Orders for Camp Nursing Services* (15¢ each, American Camping Association), gives much help in formulating these.

THE CAMP NURSE

Besides professional competence, the camp nurse must have a love for youth and be willing to give her time generously but wisely in dealing not only with physical conditions but with emotional and spiritual problems. She should know how to lead a camper to Christ, for she will have opportunities open to no one else. She must be wise enough to distinguish between the lonesome child, needing love and attention, and the physically ill, though she may help both.

Her duties include the following:

1. Before camp she will study thoroughly *The Camp Nurse* (50¢, American Camping Association), an excellent presentation of her work. This should be required of every camp nurse.

2. On opening day she will greet every camper, noting any dietary or physical restrictions that need special arrangements.

3. She will give instruction in health practices to the staff during pre-camp training, and to the campers early in the camp period.

4. She is in charge of medical supplies and equipment, keeping them locked in the camp health office. This list is suggestive:

Adhesive tape

Bandages and compresses, of various sizes and types

Scissors

Splinter forceps

Tourniquet

Splints

Hot-water bottle

Ice pack

Medicine cabinet

Thermometer

Analgesics for headache, toothache, or menstrual pain

Bicarbonate of soda

Medication for poison ivy, mosquito bites

Sunburn lotion

Cathartics

Epsom salts for external use

Antiseptics and disinfectants

Hot plate
Soap
Flashlight
Enamel basins
Wastebasket

Medication for burns
Aromatic spirits of ammonia
Paper cups, towels, napkins, tissues,
bags
Inhalation compounds

5. She prepares and operates the camp infirmary, a quiet place where campers may be placed temporarily. One room should be reserved for isolation cases. Any serious cases should be sent home or placed in a hospital immediately.

6. She arranges for delivery of meal trays to infirmary patients.

7. She keeps records of all treatments given. The records are to be kept on file in the permanent camp office until the camper is 21 years old—to avoid lawsuits.

8. She develops a well-planned pattern for handling serious emergencies, knowing transportation to use, phone location, etc. She must never be without this information.

9. She sets up regular office hours. Children like attention and will be pleased to present each mosquito bite for treatment during any hour of the day. After meals is often considered a good time for scheduled office hours. When she is not in the office, a note should state where the nurse may be reached for emergencies.

10. She checks daily with counselors as to the health of each of their campers. Some nurses find that rising early and beginning rounds of cabins when the rising bell rings is best, with rounds completed by breakfast time.

11. She checks on health practices and sanitation in camp, being familiar with the ACA standards and state regulations. She reports any shortcomings to the camp director.

12. Time may be found to teach first-aid or home-nursing courses to campers. Texts recommended are American Red Cross publications: *First Aid*, 75¢; *First Aid Textbook for Juniors*, $1.00.

13. She warns counselors against giving any medication—even aspirin! This rule should be followed without exception to avoid malpractice suits. The headache of which a camper complains may be caused by a concussion from a fall he has not reported.

14. She is familiar with the camp medical insurance program and is able to explain it intelligently when needed.

8. BUSINESS MANAGEMENT

Often in short-term evangelical camps the business manager is a minister. Why should he concern himself with the diminishing supply of potatoes, mounting bills, and disposition of cooks? The answer is, of course, that each task in an evangelical camp is spiritual; there are no secular jobs. The staff is a team, winning and nurturing souls in Christ. When eternal awards are distributed, the camp business manager will receive his full quota of celestial stars. Besides, many a minister with the hidden heart of a merchant finds satisfaction in his yearly but brief entrance into the world of commerce.

The business manager needs to be efficient in detail and able to keep records and accounts; he should have ability in purchasing and finding markets, a sense of stewardship in handling money, and ability to work with others. The following aspects of camping come under his control.

THE CAMP OFFICE

The nerve center of the camp is its office. It is desirable that this provide areas for both the camp director and the business manager. In permanent camps each should have a private room. There will be clerical help as needed in large camps that operate all summer or year-around.

In the office will be found these items:

Mailbox for outgoing mail. Incoming mail is best delivered to counselors for distribution to their campers.
Lost and found department. Announcement at mealtime of these items will help reunite them with their owners.
Public-address system, if the camp philosophy permits this. In a conference-type camp, announcements of scheduled events will be made through it, and music may be played from records at appropriate times during the day.
Bulletin board inside the office or just outside.
Sports and game equipment for checking out, if another place is not provided.

Supplies for the office itself may include files for registration cards and correspondence, paper, office forms, a punch, pencil sharpener, scissors, Scotch tape, hammer, phonograph records, thumbtacks, pencils, bookkeeping needs, cash box, ruler, rubber bands, stamp pad, and stamps. In permanent camps, a typewriter and mimeograph will be a necessity.

THE BUDGET

A tentative budget will be prepared by the business manager and approved by the committee before camp. It will be based on last year's expenses, or in a new camp, it may follow one of a camp of similar pattern. It must be flexible to some degree to care for the unexpected.

There are so many varying factors affecting budget that no two camp budgets will be alike. A budget for a typical one-week church camp with mostly volunteer staff will include the following items. Percentages for items may vary widely.

Income

Campers' fees	85%
Contributions	7
Camp store	8
	100%

Disbursements

Food	35%
Maintenance and utilities (or rent)	14
Salaries or honoraria	10
Program materials	10
Travel	8
Staff training	3.5
Health	3.5
Camp store	7
Office	2
Insurance	3
Promotion and publicity	4
	100%

BOOKKEEPING

A simple system of bookkeeping is adequate. A checking account should be established for the camp. There should be receipted bills or canceled checks for all expenditures, and each payment to the camp should be receipted. All payments should be made by the business manager. The fiscal year should close as soon after camp as possible, and the books should be audited by a competent person at once.

A double-page ledger may be used with income and disbursements on separate pages. Columns for income may include: contributions, pre-registrations, camp registrations, store receipts, etc. Disbursements may include: food, travel, allowance, staff salaries, maintenance, health, program, insurance, office supplies, etc. Sample pages are given:

INCOME

DATE	REC'D FROM:	TOTAL	PRE-REGISTRA- TION FEES	CONTRI- BUTION	CAMP STORE	REGISTRA- TION FEES
5-1-63	Robert Lewis	5.00	5.00			
5-3-63	Toledo First Church	25.00		25.00		

DISBURSEMENTS

CK. NO.	DATE	PAID TO:	TOTAL	FOOD	TRAVEL	INSUR- ANCE	PRO- GRAM
56	5-10	Mary Beth Shaw	10.54		10.54		
57	5-15	Christian Camp & Conf.	55.00			55.00	
58	5-15	Light & Life Press	35.46				35.46
59	5-25	Swift & Company	97.00	97.00			

PURCHASING

All purchasing should be done by the business manager. However, if directors of program, health, maintenance, or counseling need supplies before camp, and it is preferred that they do the purchasing in areas of their specialty, this may be done. Each needs to know the amount budgeted for his area. Requests for supplies needed during camp should be made on requisition sheets, signed by the director of that area, and presented to the business manager for purchasing.

The purchaser should make it his business to know the best outlets for camp supplies, learning how to obtain these at discount. He should have on hand up-to-date catalogs of various firms. The annual edition of the *Food Forecast and Buyers' Guide,* a supplement to *Camping Magazine,* distributed usually in February, gives excellent helps in locating sources.

It is the task of the purchaser to have current information concerning procedures for obtaining government surplus—food, equipment, and supplies. The agencies to contact vary from state to state, and regulations change frequently. The county school superintendent or city school administrator in charge of hot lunches or other purchasing can supply needed addresses of governmental officials.

INSURANCE

Those with permanent camp sites will ordinarily carry all or most of these types of insurance.

> Fire
> Theft
> Public liability
> Automobile, if there are camp vehicles
> Workmen's compensation
> Health insurance for employees

If one is renting a camp site, inquiry should be made as to whether or not public liability insurance or other insurance is carried by the owners.

All camps will wish to provide accident and medical insurance for their campers and staff. Available from various reliable companies, this covers campers from time of leaving home until return at a usual cost of from five to ten cents a day. Consult your sponsoring body to see whether or not it carries a master policy which would include your camp. If not, ask the sponsor or your denominational camping headquarters to recommend a company.

Members of the Christian Camp and Conference Association find it beneficial to insure through their master medical expense policy for campers. Address: Christian Camp and Conference Association, Post Office Box 1312, San Antonio, Texas 78206.

REGISTRATION

IS PRE-REGISTRATION NECESSARY?

In many camps the day is gone when churches just send as many campers as finally were persuaded to come by the last morning. In secular camps, quotas are often full weeks before camp begins, and this situation is becoming more true in church camping. In all camps with facilities that are not expandable and a rigid number of staff, pre-registration is a necessity.

ADVANTAGES OF PRE-REGISTRATION

It gives the number of children to expect, eliminating opening day lack of sufficient counselors and facilities.

It gives funds to open camp, an advantage if little is available from last year or from the sponsoring body.

It eliminates some of the registration procedure on opening day.

If camp is limited to a certain quota, churches may be informed when their quotas are filled.

In camps with separate units, pre-registration gives a better basis for dividing camp before opening day.

REGISTRATION PROCEDURE BEFORE CAMP

The registration card should give this information: name, address, parent or guardian, home church, grade, age, sex, local church, amount of fee paid, signatures of pastor or youth director, parent, and camper. On the back of the card or on a separate information sheet these additional facts may be supplied: church affiliation, regularity of attendance, hobbies, special interests, swimming ability, previous camp attendance.

Incentives to pre-registration may be supplied by giving a discount on the fee or a camp souvenir item such as a tee shirt, souvenir book, or decal.

Registration cards may be sent along with the camp folder, or the camp folder itself may contain a registration blank. When registration opens, the camper returns the registration card with pre-registration fee. The registrar immediately sends a receipt and a letter welcoming the camper and giving any additional information needed.

Many states require pre-camp medical examinations of all campers. If this is a requirement in your state, the appropriate blanks should be sent to the camper with receipt following pre-registration. Often a physician will donate this service to a church group if arrangements are made. Forms are available from the American Camping Association, *Camper Health Examination Forms* (for boys, for girls, for staff), 2¢ each. Many camps prefer to make their own forms in consultation with their camp physician.

THE CAMP STORE

"KAMP KANTEEN" OR "SNAK-SHAK"

The camp store has become an accepted part of camp life, especially in the conference-type program. It usually is under the supervision of the business manager. Purposes differ in various camps. In some it is a refreshment stand; in others, items for sale include film, batteries, camp tee shirts and hats, souvenir items, and Christian literature. Craft and other program items are usually sold where they are used.

Every camp needs a place where campers can buy stamps, post cards, and stationery. Many feel that it is wise to provide other items, especially Christian publications. Each camp must decide on the basis of its philosophy and objectives whether it wishes to enter into more merchandising.

After visiting scores of camps from coast to coast, the authors are convinced that "refreshment stands" as such have no place in a camp for junior and junior high ages. This same judgment is being expressed more frequently in both secular and religious camping literature. Junior ages especially will spend their whole week's allowance on sweets the first day if permitted, and some camps, seemingly eager to increase their profits, do not hinder them.

Although spending may be controlled by limiting the amount of money each camper may bring, or limiting purchases for any one day, clever campers think of ways to "beat the system," and inequalities will still exist that make for unhappiness.

A better way might be to raise the camp fee a few cents a day and give a treat or two each day—on a hot afternoon an ice-cream bar or a soft drink; before bedtime fruit, a candy bar, cookies and cocoa. This could add to the thrill of camp ("Free pop, WOW!") and would be more in keeping with the goal of making camp different from city life. If an adequate diet is provided, there is no need for a "hamburger joint" on the camp site.

In any case, early youth should not be allowed to keep money in cabins. Money is surrendered the first day during registration to be placed in the *camp bank*. Camp canteen cards are provided each child. These are good for one dollar, with squares around the edge good for five or ten cents. The card is punched after each purchase. In the center is the camper's name, store number, cabin, and the amount still in the bank. The cards may be kept by the campers or they may be kept in numerical sequence in back of the counter on a large display board which has a nail or hook for each number. When a child comes to the counter, he gives his number, and when his purchase is made and his card punched, the card is returned to the display board. In using this system, if supplies are sold in more than one place, care must be taken that a child does not overdraw his account. Offerings are taken with IOU's.

Camp checkbooks from which campers write checks for purchases are well liked by campers. These furnish a record for each camper (or his parents) of all his purchases. Some camps prefer to have envelopes into which all money is placed at beginning of camp. These are filed alphabetically; the appropriate one is given to a child upon entrance in the store, returned to the file after his purchase is made. In some camps that sell supplies in different places these envelopes are kept in the counselors' hands.

INVENTORIES AND STOREROOM

There is no use spending money for a new box of lead pencils, when looking around (or checking the inventory) will reveal that nearly two gross were left from last year. To control purchasing, inventories must be kept on items such as food and kitchen equipment; office equipment, forms, and supplies; program items (crafts, waterfront, sports, etc.); health items (drugs and supplies); tools; cabin supplies (beds, etc.). A camp renting its site will not need all these.

Supervision of the storeroom is the duty of the business manager. In large camps this is a significant and vital operation in figuring camper costs per day, etc. Technical instruction in operating large storerooms is available from commercial sources for those charged with such responsibilities.

RECORDS

The following records should be kept by the business manager and filed in the permanent camp office:

From the *registrar:* enrollment records, registration blanks, registration cards, camp mailing list.

From the *dietician* or *cooks:* menus used.

From the *staff:* application blanks, contracts, payroll and work records, job descriptions, health examination sheets, and record of first-aid treatments.

Cost of food, reduced to camper-day ratio.

Names of food suppliers with comments.

FOOD MANAGEMENT

It could be either!

"Mom, the food was icky, and I'm not going back to that camp!"

"Oh, did we ever have good meals at camp. Mom, you should get some of those recipes!"

Admittedly any camp management has a well-nigh impossible task in catering to pampered appetites of today's youth. One can't please them all, all the time, but by combining knowledge of generally well-liked foods, careful menu planning, and attractiveness in serving, a high level of satisfaction may be maintained. Food is a main source of pleasure or displeasure in the camper's entire experience of camp life. Too, the food budget will make or break the camp financially for it composes 30 to 40 per cent of the camp expenses. Hence this phase of camp deserves careful planning.

PERSONNEL

In a large camp the *dietician* has a full-time job with responsibility for all kitchen activities. Some states require a licensed home economist in permanent camps. In small camps often the dietician is also the dining-hall manager. Sometimes the cook is the dietician. The specific task of the dietician is menu planning. Menus should be completed tentatively and, with the food list, in the hands of the buyer before camp. But anyone experienced in this field realizes that day-by-day factors will mean revision of menus. Utilization of leftovers is often a deciding factor in economical operation of the kitchen.

The *cooks* are a major part of camp life. Blessed is the business manager who finds congenial cooks! They need a sense of humor, a love of children, and an elastic nervous system—besides the ability to put out attractive meals on time, often with less than the best equipment. Cheerful cooks in the kitchen add much to camp, while tense, nervous ones are a liability. Cooks need to feel that they, too, contribute to the spiritual values in camp. While campers should not be "underfoot" in the kitchen, as a cook radiates Christ in contacts with campers, often she (or he) becomes one of the most beloved of the camp staff. Definite plans should be made to give the cooks opportunity to partake in religious services.

The *handy boys* help prepare vegetables, wash cooking equipment, obtain supplies from the storeroom.

The *dining-room manager* sets up procedures for serving meals, dishwashing, and dining-room maintenance.

The *buyer* is often the business manager in smaller camps.

The *storeroom manager* has a full-time job in only the largest camps. The buyer or handy boys often take care of this responsibility in smaller camps.

The three areas of food management are *menu making, food purchasing,* and *dining-room management.*

MENU MAKING

Making of menus is the task of the dietician in cooperation with the business manager. Menus should be prepared in advance of camp, and lists of the supplies needed should be in the hands of the buyer sufficiently early to allow him time to purchase them before camp.

These factors in menu planning should be kept in mind:

1. Consider attractiveness in serving (color combinations, food consistency).

2. Know the basic foods for good nutrition. (See below.)

3. Include all classes of food daily.

4. Know availability of fresh fruits and vegetables in season. Do not be a slave to written menus.

5. Consider first the perishables in daily planning.

6. Plan combinations of foods to use small supplies and leftovers.

7. Vary method of serving and cooking when same meat or vegetable must be served on the same or a consecutive day.

8. Flavor carefully; vary seasoning.

9. Serve foods with contrasting qualities: acid and sweet, bland and highly flavored, crisp and soft, cold and hot, plain and colored.

The seven basic foods (often combined into the basic four) should be served daily:

Green and yellow vegetables, some raw, some cooked, canned, or frozen.
Oranges, tomatoes, grapefruit, some raw cabbage or salad greens.
Potatoes and other vegetables and fruits, raw, dried, cooked, frozen, or canned.
Milk and milk products.
Bread, flour, cereals, whole grain or enriched.
Meat, poultry, fish, eggs, meat substitute, peas, or beans.
Butter or vitamin A margarine.

The fundamental pattern for menus includes the following:

Breakfast	*Lunch*	*Dinner*
Fruit	Meat; fish, fowl or	Meat; fish, fowl or meat sub-
Cereal	meat substitute	stitute
Meat or egg	One vegetable	Potatoes
Bread	Dessert	Vegetables: leafy or raw
Milk or milk drink	Milk	Bread
		Dessert (fruit here or at
		noon)
		Milk

Helps to menu planning should be secured. These are suggestive sources:

1. Home economics departments of state schools. Example: New York State College of Home Economics, Cornell University, Ithaca, New York 14850. Excellent help in all phases of kitchen and dining room procedure. *Quantity Recipe File,* Iowa State University, Ames, Iowa, 50010, $8.50.
2. Wholesalers who cater to camps, schools, and institutions. Check advertisers in *Camping Magazine, Christian Camps and Conferences* (such as Kellogg's, Sexton, Gumperts, etc.). A card to them stating your desire for help in menu planning will result in a flood of mail with valuable suggestions. Example: *Camp Chow* and *Quantity Food Service for Summer Camps,* Kellogg Company, Battle Creek, Michigan 49016. New free edition each year, attractive menus, quantity recipes. See annual supplement to *Camp Magazine: Food Forecast and Buyers' Guide.*
3. Government publications. Example: *Cook Book of the U.S. Navy,* U.S. Govrenment Printing Office, Washington, D.C. 20402.
4. Firms and industrial associates. Example: National Dairy Council, 111 N. Canal Street, Chicago, Illinois 60606.

FOOD PURCHASING

Volumes have been written on this subject. Anyone in a permanent camp charged with year-around or summer-long purchasing should seek professional help. Home economists in state college home economics departments can provide sources of technical assistance in this field. Example: *Purchasing Food for Fifty* (5¢), Mailing Room, Department of Extension Teaching and Information; *Buying Food for Your Camp* (free), Food Marketing Office, both from New York State College of Agriculture, Ithaca, New York 14850.

The buyer for the short-term camp should buy wisely, considering these facts:

1. Find the best market. Compare prices of wholesale houses, a friendly retailer.

2. Know grades of canned and frozen goods and the most economical size containers.

3. Know cuts and grades of meat and determine whether it is best to buy portion cuts or whole carcasses.

4. Determine advantages of buying produce direct from farms.

5. Determine which is best in your circumstances—fresh, canned, or frozen items.

6. Keep alert to bargains in staples through the year.

7. Apply for surplus food early; keep inquiring until it is delivered; see that menus are planned to use it.

8. Always check invoices against delivery. It is easy to be shorted.

9. Keep in mind limits of storage and refrigerator space.

10. Keep these records: names of suppliers and comments on their service; menus; itemized lists of costs.

11. For daily determination of per-camper per-day costs desired in large camps, a careful system of daily inventory must be maintained. If average daily cost is desired for a short-term camp, it may be computed at the end of the period.

12. Arrange the storeroom for efficiency, placing newly purchased supplies to rear of older stock.

COOKOUTS

Food and equipment for cookouts are provided by the kitchen. Hence well-developed plans should be established by the kitchen staff for distributing and return of cookout supplies.

The office will provide a Request Sheet for Cookout Supplies. This is filled out by the counselor in charge of the cookout and turned in to the kitchen the day before supplies are needed. The sheet should give the counselor's name, date, time of leaving, time of returning, number of persons going on the cookout, food desired with type and quanity, and remarks.

Menus and methods for cookouts are readily obtainable in any campcraft book or camp program book. Free booklets on outdoor cooking are distributed by national food concerns such as Kellogg's, Battle Creek, Michigan; National Dairy Council, 111 N. Canal Street, Chicago, Illinois 60606; Stokely's, Indianapolis, Ind. 46204.

DINING-HALL MANAGEMENT

Serving meals. The dining-hall manager in a large camp is a full-time employee. In smaller camps the dietician may assume the duty of dining-room management. An early decision to be made is whether to serve meals cafeteria or family style. Much dishwashing is saved by cafeteria style, but family style is more conducive to good table manners. Some camps combine the two, serving the main dishes cafeteria style while the drink, breads, and spreads are served at the table.

Small tables with a counselor at each are recommended. Each table may have one person responsible for obtaining refills of food during the meal; another may be appointed to clear the table and reset it. These duties may be rotated. Some camps prefer to have tables served by adults or employed young people. All details of serving procedures should be explained clearly the first day of camp.

In some camps grace is said outside the dining hall if cafeteria style is used. Other camps have all seated at tables before grace. The following singing graces may be sung to the tune of the Doxology:

> We thank Thee for the morning light,
> For rest and shelter of the night,
> For health and food, for love and friends,
> For everything Thy goodness sends.   Amen.

> God is great, and God is good,
> And we thank Him for our food;
> By His hand must all be fed
> Thank you, Lord, for daily bread.   Amen.

Mealtime may make its contribution to gracious living and consideration of others, or it may be a time for careless, hurried shoveling of food from plate to mouth with little regard for others. Early in camp the dining-hall manager should discuss table manners. Youngsters easily become rowdy at mealtime unless they are impressed with the fact that quiet behavior is expected. This can be achieved with tactful firmness. One way of securing quiet for announcements is for the dining-hall manager to stand with upraised hand until all respond with the same sign.

Dishwashing. The dining-hall manager supervises dishwashing. She should be informed as to state health regulations and standards of the American Camping Association regarding this. There must be strict attention to sanitation. It is recommended that dishes be put through three waters after careful scraping, when chemical disinfectant is used. If dishes are disinfected by scalding, rinse water must be a minimum of 170 degrees, with dishes left in it for two minutes. Drying in racks is preferred to drying with towels. If campers wash dishes, careful supervision must be given to see that dishes are washed clean with all grease removed. If dishes are towel-dried, provision must be made to wash the towels daily or send them to a laundry.

In some conference-type camps, dishwashing is done by electricity, with employees scraping and putting dishes away. In more informal camping, campers assist—it being thought by management that campers need to have camp duties. On the basis of camp philosophy and careful compliance with sanitary regulations, each camp must decide its own pattern.

Washing of pots and pans is under supervision of the cooks and is done by handy boys. This should never be used as punishment for it tends to punish the cooks more than the miscreant.

9. DENOMINATIONAL DIRECTION

Executives in denominations or youth organizations who have the responsibility for camping can do much to inspire better camping practices. True, camping usually begins at the grass roots. But the grass-root operators usually are groping for better methods and gladly accept leadership that is tactfully and wisely given. While some denominations have yet to center authority for camping in any headquarters board or executive, there seems to be a feeling that this should be done. Certainly if coordination of camping effort is desired, there must be some direction from the top level.

The following are areas in which a denominational camping program may be strengthened by headquarter's direction and guidance:

1. Gathering annual reports from all camps to ascertain what is being done; tabulating them to chart advances and note weaknesses.
2. Initiating legislation to provide in the denomination's manual of government an official place for camping in the church structure, establishing a department of camping, setting up a director of camping on the general church level; on lower levels providing for regional, conference, or district directors with voice and vote in boards of Christian education (or comparable bodies) for their level.
3. Publishing camping literature. Some denominations have periodic mailing of helpful materials to all camp directors. Some publish their own camp manuals and camp Bible curriculum.
4. Recommending helpful books. Reviews of camping books should appear in book review columns of the church periodical. A list of recommended books for libraries in the district or region should be made available.
5. Publishing camp statistics, news items, human-interest articles, etc., in church periodicals, keeping camping before the denomination. These provide a spur or inspiration for others to begin or improve camps in their areas.

6. Scheduling camping workshops at Sunday-school conventions, conferences, general gatherings.
7. Urging church colleges and other schools to schedule camping courses in their curriculum.
8. Setting up a leadership training course in camping under the official church training program with credit toward whatever certificates may be given in the denomination. This volume is prepared for such usage in evangelical churches.
9. Urging cooperation with existing camp agencies and partaking of their benefits: ACA, NSSA Camp Commission, CCA, etc.
10. Establishing standards for camps within the organization, assisting in every possible way the meeting of these standards by individual camps.

BIBLIOGRAPHY

The following books for further study in the field of camp administration are arranged in recommended order of purchase for the average evangelical camp. See bibliographies listed in Appendix for further related publications.

ACA Camp Standards. Martinsville, Ind.: American Camping Association, 1956. 10¢.

Dimock, Hedley (editor). *Administration of the Modern Camp.* New York: Association Press, 1948. $4.00.

Yearbook of Christian Camping; and *Ideas Unlimited.* Van Nuys, Calif.: Christian Camp and Conference Association, annual editions. Special prices to members of CCA. (Evangelical in emphasis.)

Special Committee on Camps and Conferences of the Division on Christian Education, NCCCA. *Church Camping for Junior Highs.* Philadelphia: Westminster Press, 1960. $1.50.

Camp Director's Handbook. Wheaton, Ill.: Scripture Press, 1959. 50¢. (Evangelical in emphasis.)

Reimann, Lewis C. *The Successful Camp.* Ann Arbor, Mich.: University of Michigan Press, 1958. $4.75.

Ledlie, John A. *Managing the YMCA Camp.* New York: Association Press, 1961. $4.95.

Administration of Girl Scout Camps. Girl Scouts of America, $1.95.

Camp Management. New Brunswick, N. J. Boy Scouts of America, 1966. 60¢.

FOR COMMITTEES

Understanding How Groups Work (Leadership Pamphlet No. 4). Chicago: Adult Education Association of the U.S.A., 332 S. Michigan 60604, 1956. 60¢.

Trecker, Audrey and Harleigh. *Committee Common Sense*. New York: Association Press. $2.95.

STUDY HELPS

1. Who should be included in planning of the camp program?
2. What subcommittees are suggested for camp program planning?
3. What are basic qualities of a good camp director?
4. State advantages and disadvantages of having maintenance under the business manager; of having counselors do all instructional work.
5. In your ideal camp what would be your decisions as to age, sex, size, date, duration? Give reasons.
6. Name aspects of publicity and promotion which you consider most important.
7. What are the ACA, CCA, NSSA Camp Commission?
8. What are the reasons for follow-up and evaluation in camping?
9. In your ideal camp what kind of camp store would you have?
10. Why must a nurse have "standing orders" from a physician?
11. Name duties of the camp business manager.
12. Give two reasons why food is so important at camp.
13. What are the three areas of food management?
14. How may camps profit from denominational or organizational guidance?

PROJECTS

1. Draw a camp organizational chart of either an actual or an ideal camp.
2. Design a camp promotional folder.
3. Design a camp evaluation sheet for campers.
4. Construct a week's menu for a junior high camp.

IV. WHERE TO DO IT?

SITE — FACILITIES — SAFETY — SANITATION

"The joy of playing in healthful mud, of paddling in clean water, of hearing roosters call up the sun, and birds sing praises to God for the new day . . .

"The vision of pure skies enriched at dawn and sunset with unspeakable glory; of dew-drenched mornings flashing with priceless gems; of grain-fields and woodlands yielding to the feet of the wind; of the vast sky 'all throbbing and panting with stars' . . .

"To live with flowers and butterflies, with the wild things that have made possible the world of fable.

"To experience the thrill of going barefoot, of being out in the rain without umbrellas and rubber coats and buckled overshoes; of riding a white birch, or sliding down pine-boughs, of climbing ledges and tall trees; of diving head first into a transparent pool.

"To know the smell of wet earth, of new-mown hay, of blossoming wild grape and eglantine . . . of the crushed leaves of wax myrtle, sweet-fern, mint and fir; of the breath of cattle and of fog blown in from the sea.

"To hear the answer the trees make to the rain, and to the wind; the sound of rippling and falling water; the muffled roar of the sea in storm, and its lisping and laughing and clapping of hands in a stiff breeze. . . .

"To catch fish, to ride on a load of hay, to camp out, cook over an open fire, tramp through new country and sleep under the open sky. To have the fun of driving and riding a horse, paddling a canoe, sailing a boat, and of discovering that nature will honor the humblest seed they plant." [1]

Good camp sites help children claim this birthright!

[1] Henry Turner Bailey, in Kenneth Webb (editor), *Light from a Thousand Campfires* (New York: Association Press, 1960), p. 101.

10. SELECTING THE SITE

In beginning a new camp for early youth, the committee must early decide, "Where shall our camp site be?" There are three possibilities: to rent, buy, or use the present church or denominational conference grounds.

Renting has these advantages (which may also be disadvantages of owning): (1) escape from the initial cost of investment and later upkeep; (2) escape from the labor involved in building and maintaining, preparing annually for camp; (3) ease of relocation to fit changing needs; (4) ready availability of well-developed camps that have proper facilities for camping of early youth.

These are advantages of *buying* (which may also be disadvantages of renting): (1) ease of scheduling to fit one's own needs instead of the owner's schedule, and security in using the site year after year; (2) building of a spirit of morale in the sponsoring body through camp site development—a work project; (3) possibility of consciously planning for and (eventually) realizing the type of camping desired; (4) application of camp fees (which continue to spiral) to purchasing own site instead of paying for another's.

Church committees which have *regular denominational conference or camp grounds* may have use of these at a reduced per diem rate or for payment merely of utilities costs. But accepting this solution is not always the best decision. Conference grounds often lack facilities for true camping and outdoor living, located as many of them are in populous areas away from waterfront or attractive settings. If the available camp site is not what the committee desires, it is well within its rights to seek another site.

Those who must use existing facilities that have serious drawbacks must take an imaginative approach. Good camping experiences may still be given if the camp staff is creative and refuses to be bound by sameness in camp programming.

PURCHASING THE SITE

Having decided that a new site is to be purchased, the committee must formulate some basic policies before it begins to look at real estate:

1. Where is financial support to come from? What funds are available immediately? What may be raised later? What is the top price to pay for a site?

2. What is the potential number of campers and groups to be served?

3. What type of camping is desired and what facilities are needed for this?

4. How many buildings are needed?

5. What is the approximate acreage of the site?

With these basic decisions made, the actual searching begins. No property should be purchased without considering each of these factors:

1. Is it suitable for the purposes of the camp program, campers, and age groups to be served?

2. Is it a place of beauty, located near hills, mountains, a lake or a beach, with something to give natural enchantment to the site?

3. Is it away from population centers or thoroughfares to insure privacy and avoid distractions? What other developments or roads are planned in this area?

4. Is there an adequate water supply? Is fuel accessible? Is there electric power, telephone, milk and mail delivery, fire protection?

5. Is there adequate drainage for sanitary facilities and to avoid dampness?

6. Is there adequate acreage available for future needs? Do not underestimate this possibility. Recommended is one acre per camper to allow for outdoor living experiences.

7. Is the area free from flood danger? Are there other natural hazards—cliffs, quicksand, poisonous snakes or vines?

8. Is it readily accessible and centrally located for all who use it?

9. Does it have possibilities that will allow the health and safety requirements of your area and camping standards to be met?

10. Are there trees to provide shade and free area for play?

11. What are local regulations regarding zoning, building, etc.?

12. Is it adjacent to state or national parks whose facilities may be used to give expanded camping experiences?

13. Can you obtain a clear title to the property?

No perfect site will be found, but some weaknesses will be so serious as to merit rejection of the site; others may be corrected. Do not take the word of a salesman on important matters (no matter how trustworthy). His information may be hearsay. Seek professional advice before buying.

❧❧❧❧❧❧❧❧

11. DEVELOPING THE SITE

THE MASTER PLAN

The initial step in development of a camp of any size is mapping the area. A topographical map with contour lines showing elevation will give a clear picture of natural conditions. This is best made professionally by a local surveyor, whose fee will be a good investment in any extensive camp. Maps other than contour may be made by talented staff members or older campers.

The topographical map becomes the basis of the master plan, which projects the camp as it will be when completed. A civil engineer should be consulted as to roads, water supplies, sewage disposal, etc. Architects will be needed in developing camp layout, designing buildings in harmony with the site, and meeting state and local codes.

The master plan will be broken down into immediate and long-range objectives, to be accomplished over a five-year period. As constituents see the map and the five-year plan, interest in contributing labor and finances is more easily aroused. The first year should see essential utilities and sanitation needs installed, as well as the dining hall and kitchen. These then follow as rapidly as possible: cabins, swimming facilities, shower houses, infirmary, chapel, staff quarters, office, storage, dock, boathouses, etc.

BUILDINGS AND FACILITIES

The committee must make clear to the engineers and architects the philosophy and objectives of the camp, explaining the particular kind of camping desired. Further factors are then to be taken into consideration in planning specific kinds and location of buildings and facilities:

1. Local health regulations and camping standards.
2. Water supply and sanitation plans.
3. Fire control.
4. Weather, sun and shade, prevailing winds.
5. Relationship with other buildings, and harmony with the site.
6. Natural features (in building placement); conservation factors.
7. Immediate cost compared to long-range maintenance.
8. Adaptation to other use and for year-around use.
9. Effect on public relations. (Will it be considered "too fancy"? etc.).
10. Compatibility with long-range plan. "Temporary" structures often have a long life.
11. Safety regulations as given in ACA and other camp standards.

LIVING FACILITIES

The philosophy of the camp, and the weather will largely determine the type of living quarters. Some camp directors prefer nothing more civilized than canvas quarters; other "camps" offer rooms with maid service. The majority of camps for early youth now have enclosed cabins. If they are designed for summer use only, they are screened instead of windowed. The tendency is away from placing cabins in rows and toward arranging them in units or villages, each with its own lodge and washhouse. Cabins should be light and airy, affording sufficient room for each camper to have a shelf with storage space under it for hanging clothes. Four campers per room is considered ample in junior camps, eight in junior high camps. Two-story buildings are discouraged. Forty square feet per camper is recommended, with six feet between side rails of beds and four feet between end rails. Double-deck beds are not recommended. Anyone who has counseled where these are used can easily understand why. Many camps furnish only cots, requiring the camper to bring a bedroll or sleeping bag. Others supply cots, mattresses, and sometimes blankets and linens. Boy and Girl Scout camps do not permit electricity in living quarters.

In warm, arid climates tents are acceptable. Even where rain is not unusual a well-constructed frame for tent and fly is adequate, and a tent gives more camping atmosphere.

Some camps insist that counselors sleep in the same room with campers; others feel that counselors should have some privacy. Counselors' rooms in a unit arrangement are usually separate from the campers'. Cooks should have quarters separate from the kitchen area; the nurse should have her bedroom in the infirmary. Caretaker and camp director in permanent camps have residences on the site. Other staff cabins are provided as necessary. Every camp should have an area where the staff may "escape" from the campers. This rest area is out of bounds for campers.

Latrines should be built near sleeping facilities. Earth-pit latrines can be satisfactory and not a health hazard if built according to government specifications, carefully ventilated, screened, and limed and cleaned daily. Flush toilets require an adequate supply of running water and sewage disposal. One toilet seat for every ten persons is recommended. All latrines should be lighted at night and partitioned for privacy.

Handwashing facilities are to be provided in proximity to toilets. Industrial-type lavatories of metal with several faucets (each camper having his own basin and towels) are recommended as being more sanitary than the regular washbowls. Hot-water showers are necessary in some states to meet health regulations, with one shower head for every twenty persons. Gang showers are rising in popularity, but private showers should be provided for the staff and for campers requesting them.

THE KITCHEN AND DINING HALL

This is probably considered the most important building in camp.

While campers may enjoy primitive sleeping quarters, the kitchen should have every convenience the budget can allow. It has areas for

Delivery of supplies	Washing of dishes and pots and pans
Food preparation	Cleaning materials
Cooking	Garbage disposal
Serving	Dining facilities for kitchen staff
Storage and refrigeration	Toilet space for staff
Sink for hand washing	Dietician's desk

Each of these areas should be in proper relationship arranged for maximum efficiency. Expert advice should be secured in purchasing ranges, hot-water heaters, and dishwashers to obtain the correct size for the camp enrollment. Dishwashing facilities must provide for scalding of dishes in 170° hot water for two minutes or disinfecting with chemicals. Dishes should be stored in closed closets. Plastic dishes and stainless steel table utensils are becoming popular. Publications of state and federal health departments give much assistance in planning for kitchen sanitation.

Cement floors are required under stoves but should be tiled where workers stand.

There are many plans available for kitchen and dining-room areas. The T shape is a favored one, with dining area to either side of the kitchen. If the building is to be used in winter, thought must be given to heating smaller areas. Large windows allowing much light are desirable. Both kitchen and dining room must be screened. A fireplace in the dining room is popular, especially when the room is used for assemblies or as a recreation area on rainy days.

ADMINISTRATION AREA

The administration area should be closest to the entrance. It includes the office and store, infirmary, staff houses, and parking area. Office space requirements vary with individual camps. The store may be a room in the office, but with a separate outside entrance. The infirmary provides, besides sleeping quarters for the nurse, her office, a ward, a bathroom, an isolation room with outside entrance. Staff houses vary from modern residences for permanent staff to simple sleeping cabins with no washing and toilet facilities.

PROGRAM FACILITIES

Few parts of the camp program have the appeal of *waterfront* activities. Some camps center their program so much in these that they cannot conceive of a camp without them, though many such camps exist. There are these types of swimming facilities:

Ocean. Usable only at certain tides and not in places of heavy surf.

Rivers. Used only if unpolluted, and with provisions made to avoid strong currents and drop-offs.

Lakes. Must be tested for pollution and any contamination eliminated.

Artificial lakes. Constructed only after consultation with a civil engineer to determine whether turnover of water volume is sufficient to insure sanitation. "Mud holes" are not safe swimming areas.

Artificial pools.

Swimming pools should be constructed in well-drained areas, never in a low spot. They must be built under professional advice. Rectangular pools are most economical and simplest. The pool should be fenced and away from trees, the surface skimmed and bottom vacuumed daily, the water adequately chlorinated. Showers are required before swimmers enter the pool.

Any swimming areas should be divided into three divisions, clearly marked: non-swimmers, not deeper than 3'6"; intermediate, not over 7'; swimming and diving area, not less than 7'. For each swimmer fifty square feet of water is desirable, and ten square feet is a minimum. The bottom of any natural swimming area should be cleared of debris and filled in with sand.

Docks of the H or A type are recommended. Floats, lifeguard tower, platform, cribs, diving boards, and lifesaving equipment should follow safety specifications. Boating docks may be adjacent to the swimming area but must be separate. Boathouses and racks for canoes are added as desired. Growth of algae and water plants must be controlled in some areas. Copper sulfate is often recommended, though more modern chemicals advertised in camping magazines are available. All state and safety regulations for boating must be strictly followed, with adult supervision in each boat, and each non-swimmer equipped with a life belt. Red Cross and YMCA publications should be studied by all waterfront personnel.

Nature areas are an important consideration in camp site planning. Some area should be left in the natural state for sheer enjoyment of the wild woods, for instructional purposes, and to furnish materials for nature crafts. A trail through the area may be developed, with nature items marked and a nature museum at its entrance.

Some area of the camp or in the adjoining wilderness should be the outpost camping location—for cookouts and overnight camping.

Rifle ranges are ideally located at the foot of a hill not less than thirty feet to the crest. All safety regulations must be met, including fencing in of sides.

Archery ranges may be set up in any suitable open area, using four-foot targets with 50-foot range. Increasingly popular are field archery courses with various kinds of targets, scoring as in golf. All safety factors must be observed.

In evangelical camping the *chapel* is the most sacred spot of the camp. It should be in a scenic location, with a worshipful atmosphere. Seating should be comfortable but not elaborate. In suitable climates the chapel may be a natural outdoor amphitheater or it may be located in a woods. Sometimes it is only a roof supported by poles, with open sides. In colder and damper climates an enclosed structure is a necessity. This should be kept as rustic as possible.

A small prayer chapel in a choice scenic spot provides a retreat for private meditation or counseling. It can become one of the most cherished places in camp.

The campfire or council ring provides an informal gathering place. Often the outdoor fireplace has benches arranged in a circle around it.

Shelters for special activities must not be forgotten. In a warm climate, craft houses and those used for special purposes may be open structures. They should provide tables and benches, and storage space as needed. Classes in Christian living in evangelical camps in warm climates may meet outdoors entirely without shelters, but housing must be provided in colder climates and for rainy days. To be avoided are classrooms similar to those used in Sunday school.

SPECIAL FACILITIES

Every permanent camp needs a workshop where tools are kept and repair jobs done. This is the headquarters of the maintenance crew and should be equipped as well as the camp program demands. A garage is a necessity in permanent camps with vehicles. Separate storage buildings are required in camps where sleeping quarters are not enclosed to store mattresses, tents, etc., in dry, rodent-proof areas. If the camp is closed all winter, often the dining hall is used for storage.

UTILITIES

The rule for *roads* in camp is "as few as possible." From the access road the first thing to greet those coming to the camp site is the entrance. This should be attractively designed of stone or log materials marked with the camp name. The entrance road from gateway to administration area should be as short as possible, friendly in appearance, conserving the natural atmosphere. This road terminates at the visitors' parking lot. A service road open to service vehicles only extends to the kitchen area. Other roads, to the craft area, for example, are kept closed except for deliveries. The parking area should be ample for staff cars, buses, and visitors, with room for overflow on special occasions. It is best kept as natural looking as possible, without blacktop or other paving.

Paths and trails between areas of the camp should be planned as needed. Signs designating areas on buildings should be rustic in design so as to add to the attractiveness of the camp. Directional signs on approaching roads should be posted as necessary and conform to highway regulations.

Water supply is vital to a camp. The quantity of water needed depends on the camp program. Primitive camps with pit privies may estimate requirements at 10 to 30 gallons per day per person. Camps with swimming pool, dishwasher, fountains, showers, and flush toilets may need 50 to 80 gallons per day per person. Sources of water are: *springs* (should be enclosed), *dug wells* (should be enclosed), *drilled or driven wells* (preferred), *surface water* (must be chlorinated).

All water must be tested frequently, and local health rules must be observed. Technical assistance should be sought for installation of any extensive water system requiring electric pumphouse, water tower, or chlorinator. Bubbler fountains should be provided in convenient locations.

Electricity brought into camp from adjacent power lines should be installed in the manner advised by the engineer of the power company. All wiring in buildings must conform to local codes. In areas far removed from power lines a generator may be desirable, either AC for standard appliances or DC for smaller and specially equipped ones.

SEWAGE DISPOSAL

Even if pit latrines are used, waste water from kitchen and showers must be disposed of. Cesspools may be used, though they are not recommended. With these it is necessary to have a grease trap, frequently cleaned, on kitchen drains. Septic tanks are better and can care also for sanitary sewage. These should be built with professional advice, the drainfield being well below the level of the water source. Some large camps now are required to install commercial-type sewage disposal systems.

REFUSE AND GARBAGE

All combustible materials should be burned. Cans and bottles may be flattened or broken before burial. Garbage is best hauled from the camp site to a regular disposal location. If it must be kept on the ground, it should be buried in fly-tight pits or dirt-covered furrows. Burning of garbage requires special incinerators constructed with professional advice. The garbage can area in camp should be kept clean and orderly, scrubbed daily, not allowed to become a fly-infested or odoriferous place.

TELEPHONE

Every camp must have access to a nearby telephone. In camps for early youth, campers are not allowed to use the telephone except in emergencies. Installations in camp should be made in the office, infirmary, and kitchen. Camps used for adults will have pay booths.

LAUNDRY

Only the largest camps have laundry facilities. Long-term camps may provide a place for the camp staff to do laundry, though most camps will have it sent out. In short-term camps laundry facilities for campers are not necessary. Kitchen towels, potholders, etc., may be sent out or done in the camp laundry if there is one.

FIRE PREVENTION

A well-thought-out method of coping with fire should be a part of every camp plan. It will include everything from smothering grease fires in the kitchen to mapping escape routes from major forest fires. Instruction in behavior in case of fire should be included in pre-camp training. Buildings and equipment should be planned and maintained in accordance with good fire prevention practices. ACA standards in fire prevention should be met.

12. MAINTENANCE

The director is responsible for maintenance and works out the maintenance schedule with his employees—the caretaker and assistants. A long-range plan of maintenance should be developed. In most camps one person can manage the task, but in large camps a superintendent and crew are kept busy. These staff members should be sympathetic to the religious objectives of the camp, feeling that their work, too, contributes to the spiritual benefits of the campers.

A maintenance manual for each camp may be profitably compiled listing all the tasks to be done at specified times of the year. The following list is suggestive only; it should be amplified in detail.

BEFORE CAMP

1. Check all buildings for needed repairs or replacements: windows, screens, steps, floorboards, roofs, downspouts, chimneys and flues. See that floors are swept and scrubbed and hinges oiled.

2. Remove leaves and debris in sleeping area; inspect and repair cots, springs; air bedding. Pitch tents as needed.

3. In the dining hall clean tables, chairs, ranges, kitchen machines, refrigerators, stoves, and compressors. Check operation of kitchen machines. Wash dishes and discard chipped or cracked ones; seal or mop floors.

4. Remove rubbish and fallen trees from camp grounds. Repair roads; replace unsightly signs. Clean ditches and culverts; check bridges.

5. Remove debris from swimming area. Return boats and docks, etc., to water after checking, repairing, and painting as needed. Put lifesaving equipment in place; clean pool and check pool equipment.

6. Spray for insect infestation; make plans for rodent control; remove poisonous plants.

7. Check all utilities—telephone and electric lines, all electrical equipment such as pump, motors, chlorinator. Test plumbing for leaks and winter damage; check sewage disposal.

DURING CAMP

Maintenance tasks must be well defined during camp according to the camp philosophy. Some camps require campers to help in various ways as part of their training and camp experience. In other camps all tasks remain the duty of maintenance crews or other service personnel. Each camp must set up its own pattern, which should be written out in detail for a clear understanding by all concerned. Responsibility for each of these tasks and others as necessary should be pinpointed: cleaning kitchen and dining room, craft houses, chapel, office, etc.; cleaning latrines, wash and shower houses; laundering kitchen towels, etc.; disposing of garbage and emptying of trash cans; and cleaning pool and waterfront.

AFTER CAMP

1. Check buildings carefully, again noting painting and repair jobs to be done before winter.
2. Store all equipment, discarding items beyond repair.
3. Cover with rust preventive any metal equipment in kitchen. Clean and grease motor-driven machines; clean refrigerator, garbage containers, etc.
4. In freezing climates prepare plumbing, disconnecting and draining.
5. Remove docks, boats, cribs, etc., from water to storage.
6. Clean pool, shower houses.
7. Dry tents thoroughly before storage in rodent-proof place.
8. Prepare inventory of supplies and equipment as requested by the director.

◇◇◇◇◇◇◇◇

13. CONSERVATION IN CAMP

Some camps wear out their camp sites in a few decades because of poor conservation practices. Erosion of soil leaves tree roots exposed; gullies appear; grass and native vegetation cease to grow under tramping of many feet; dust and mud make walking unpleasant; trees are cut indiscriminately; natural beauty is defaced by ugly and unnecessary roads having no regard to scenic value; no saplings remain for camp crafts; wildlife has fled.

On the other hand, a camp may have purchased a site that has drawbacks but through careful conservation practices restored much of its former beauty. These involve planting trees to form buffer areas, to block off encroachment of outside developments, and to provide windbreaks or shelterbreaks for wildlife; planting hedges to shield unsightly areas; sowing grass in open areas where there is foot traffic; preventing erosion by building diversion terraces on hillsides where there is serious water runoff; stabilizing stream banks; draining marshy areas; grassing in or filling in erosion gullies with heavy equipment.

Poor conservation in camps often comes through overuse—too many people on the camp site. Much of it is the result of lack of awareness on the part of the camp committee as to the importance of conservation. Each camp committee should be dedicated to the task of saving the natural beauty of the camp site, allowing no practice which defaces it unnecessarily. Conservation should begin as soon as the site is purchased; all buildings and roads should be placed with due regard to conservation practices.

BIBLIOGRAPHY

The following books for further study in development of the camp site are arranged in recommended order of purchase for the average evangelical camp. See bibliographies listed in Appendix for further related publications.

ACA Camp Standards. Martinsville, Ind.: American Camping Association, 1956. 10¢.

Salomon, Julian H. *Camp Site Development.* New York: Girl Scouts, $3.00.

Camp Sites and Facilities. Brunswick, N.Y.: Boy Scouts of America, 1967. $7.50.

Organized Camp Site and Facilities. Boy Scouts of America, 1966. 60¢.

YMCA. *Developing Camp Sites and Facilities.* New York: Association Press, $3.50.

Conservation of the Campsite. Martinsville, Ind.: American Camping Association, 1960. 75¢.

STUDY HELPS

1. What are the advantages of renting and of buying a camp site?
2. What are some factors to consider in selecting a camp site?
3. How is a master plan developed?
4. What do you consider to be ideal living facilities for junior and junior high ages in camps with your climate?
5. What are the usual areas, buildings, and facilities to be planned for a new camp site?
6. What areas should be included in a kitchen?
7. What are the usual sources of water supply? How should each be safeguarded?
8. In the camps with which you are most familiar, who is in charge of maintenance?
9. What tasks of maintenance would you assign to campers during camp?
10. What conservation methods should be practiced at camp?

PROJECTS

1. Draw a master plan for an ideal camp, or for your own camp, showing desired development to make it more ideal.

V. WHO'LL DO IT?

CAMPERS — STAFF

There's something about being with people who give themselves to organized camping that is downright enchanting. No matter in which camp they are found, they'll be the same—happy, genial folks, with whom fellowship is a delight—from the keen young waterfront director to the jolly cooks, who delight to stuff the staff; from the patient genius with graying hair in the craft house to the generalissimo himself, the "super" camp director.

The reason is, of course, that camping attracts persons who have learned how to live. They have found the secret of a satisfying life—giving themselves in service to others. They've risen beyond living the crowded, cramped, uncomfortable life of being all wrapped up in oneself. Friendly and outgoing, they have found their life pattern in consideration for others. This unselfish spirit results in a charm and cordiality that can't help but form the basis for gratifying friendships.

Then, too, they are interesting people with something to share. First, of course, in Christian camping, their thought is to share Christ, which they proceed to do with a winsome, winning spirit. But beyond this they have enmeshed themselves in a variety of hobbies—from fly tying to star gazing—for which they have a missionary zeal, eager to motivate others to widen their horizons.

The grumps, the grouches, the complainers are seldom to be found at camp.

And after camp is over, and the years stretch on, in retrospect will stand out those happiest days of fellowship spent with kindred spirits—those wonderful folks who make up camp staffs.

14. THE CAMPER (EARLY YOUTH)

UNDERSTANDING HIM

They come streaming into camp the first morning from the buses and cars—campers in a variety of shapes, sizes, and dispositions. The challenge that wells up in the hearts of the waiting staff members is to learn to know these eager ones as individuals—each one's hopes, joys, problems, successes.

While they vary physically, they are all alike in one way: each has an immortal soul that needs to be won to Christ. This is the challenge of the evangelical camp staff member—to understand each as an individual, establishing rapport that the Holy Spirit might work through the staff, accomplishing His purposes in the camper. God has ordained the use of human instrumentalities in reaching others. Campers will be won to Him during camp as the staff works effectively according to God's patterns.

The first task, then, is understanding the camper. From the camp information sheet and from informal conversation these facts should be gleaned:

1. Background: his home, his school achievements, the socioeconomic level of his family, the cultural pattern of the home.
2. His personal traits: experiences, abilities, interests.
3. Reasons for coming to camp: parents' desire, his own.

Helpful to the counselor is knowledge of the age characteristics of early youth. The following listing by Lloyd Mattson presents these for junior (preadolescent) and junior high (early adolescent) ages on a departmental basis. For a serious study in this field, a graded approach, giving characteristics for each year, is also recommended. (See the Bibliography at the end of Part V.)

AGE CHARACTERISTICS OF EARLY YOUTH [1]

Junior (Ages 9-12)	*Junior High* (Ages 12-15)

PHYSICAL

Growth slows, increased endurance	Rapid growth causing self
Loves activity, exuberant	consciousness
Greater coordination	Spurts of energy or fatigue
Likes outdoors, camping	Puzzled by awareness of sex
Growing sense of independence	drives
Frequently untidy	Boys attain puberty
Peak of health period	Improved coordination, love of
Girls frequently attain puberty	sports

MENTAL

Reads, writes well	Unstable emotional life
Golden period of memorization	Frequently critical, hasty
Improved concepts of cause-effect,	judgments
time-space	Tends to indulge in self-worship-
Curiosity about who and how	ing day dreams
Increasing powers of concentration	Wishes to make decisions govern-
Reasoning powers developing	ing his actions
Interest in nature, collecting	Active sense of humor
Mounting creative ability	Given to moodiness
Keen mental ability	

SOCIAL

Growing social consciousness	Follow-the-crowd spirit, gang
Demands justice, fair play	loyalty
Enjoys group activity, gang loyalty	Craves status, self importance
Hero-worships adults	Desires to be grown up
Indifference to opposite sex	Hungers for reality, feigns
Decreasing shyness	indifference
Capable of recognizing authority	Wants to act as he pleases
Age of social awakening	Attracted to opposite sex
	Transfers loyalty to hero

[1] Lloyd D. Mattson, *Camping Guideposts* (Chicago: Moody Press, 1963), p. 16.

Junior (Ages 9-12)	Junior High (Ages 12-15)
SPIRITUAL	
Capable of meaningful decision for salvation or dedication	Questions his faith: wants to know the why and how, susceptible to counsel of unbelievers
Questions spiritual teachings	
Capable of Bible study, personal devotions	Hungers for guidance, leans on older young people, craves assurance
Open to challenge to spiritual growth	
Interest in others leads to interest in soul winning	Unstable in spiritual temper
	Capable of deep spiritual experiences

THE BASIC EMOTIONAL NEEDS OF CHILDREN

Camp staff members should be aware of the basic needs of children. It is the privilege of staff members as parent substitutes for the camp term to supply these needs as far as possible in the camping situation. But it is a higher privilege to explain to the camper (especially the one from an insecure home situation) that God and His Church meet every need of the human heart. Even if the parents and home life cannot provide the elements listed below, God can and will. The insecure camper can leave camp with a new sense of security as this truth of God's love is opened to him.

The following list is compiled by the National Association for Mental Health, a secular organization. Evangelicals may differ with it in the items after which bracketed comments are inserted.

WHAT EVERY CHILD NEEDS

To grow healthy and strong, children should have good food, plenty of sleep, exercise and fresh air. Children have emotional needs, too. To have perfect health—to be both healthy and happy—all children require . . .

Love. Every child needs to feel
　that his parents love, want and enjoy him
　that he matters very much to someone
　that there are people near to him who care what happens to him

Acceptance. Every child needs to believe
　that his parents like him for himself, just the way he is

that they like him all the time, and not only when he acts according to
their ideas of the way a child should act

that they always accept him, even though often they may not approve
of the things he does

that they will let him grow and develop in his own way [Evangelical
parents will give careful guidance.]

Security.   Every child needs to know
that his home is a good safe place he can feel sure about

that his parents will always be on hand, especially in times of crisis
when he needs them most

that he belongs to a family or group; that there is a place where he
fits in

Protection.   Every child needs to feel
that his parents will keep him safe from harm

that they will help him when he must face strange, unknown and fright-
ening situations

Independence.   Every child needs to know
that his parents want him to grow up and that they encourage him to
try new things

that they have confidence in him and in his ability to do things for himself and by himself

Faith.   Every child needs to have
a set of moral standards to live by

a belief in the human values—kindness, courage, honesty, generosity
and justice [Evangelical faith includes belief in God and His truths.]

Guidance.   Every child needs to have
friendly help in learning how to behave toward persons and things
grown-ups around him who show him by example how to get along
with others

Control.   Every child needs to know
that there are limits to what he is permitted to do and that his parents
will hold him to these limits

that though it is all right to feel jealous or angry, he will not be allowed
to hurt himself or others when he has these feelings [Evangelicals
cannot condone wrong attitudes but seek deliverance from these
through conversion experiences.]

Children whose basic needs are satisfied have a better chance to grow up in good mental health and to become mentally healthy adults—people who are good parents, good mates, good workers, good neighbors, good citizens.[2]

BEHAVIOR PROBLEMS

When these basic needs of children are not met, it is to be expected that poor behavior symptoms will occur. These include

Frustrations	Fantasy
Fears	Selfishness
Crying	Cowardliness
Aggression	Stubbornness
Lethargy	Sense of failure
Boredom	Lack of self-respect
Nervousness	Restlessness
Seclusiveness	Timidity

These are normal reactions, are to be expected, and do not as such constitute problems, but when they lead to overt acts that are anti-social, then behavior problems have emerged.

PROBLEMS OF EXCESSIVE TEMPERAMENT

Temper tantrums	Disobedience
Showing off	Destructiveness
Bullying	Obscene language
Teasing	Lying
Fighting	Stealing

In dealing with these behavior problems, it is to be borne in mind that they occur because of underlying causes which the staff member will try to understand, though it is not expected that camp staff members will be professional psychiatrists. Good common sense will help discover the reasons for much misbehavior.

Particular methods of dealing with these problems are given in books on guidance. (See Bibliography at the end of Part V.) But the evangelical counselor has an effective means of handling them,

[2] *What Every Child Needs* (pamphlet, National Association for Mental Health, Inc., 10 Columbus Circle, New York 19, N.Y.).

using the religious approach rather than the psychological. Various misbehaviors can be pointed out in Bible verses as displeasing to God. The camper should be led to see that they are sins in God's sight. They may be confessed to God, His forgiveness sought, and His strength used in overcoming them. The boy who indulges in temper tantrums can learn to curb them through prayer and depending on God for strength. Many a Christian with a former violent temper can testify to this miracle. Conversion and a godly Christian walk provide relief from wrong attitudes.

CRUSHES

Early youth is the age of hero worship. A camper-staff member crush should be treated in a matter-of-fact way by the staff member, who thanks the camper for the compliment, letting him know that this is common; then the matter is dropped.

Camper-camper crushes are to be expected, especially in junior high camping. They are not encouraged but accepted as normal, with controls set that will minimize interference with the camp program.

(Staff-staff crushes have often developed into lifelong romances, a delightful by-product of Christian camping.)

HOMESICKNESS

Nearly every camp has to face the problem of what to do with the homesick camper. The following is a list of some reasons for homesickness. The case must be diagnosed and treated appropriately.

Being over-attached to parents, chums, or pets back home
Longing for customary amusements
Lack of privacy
Disliking work assignments
Lacking ability to participate in group activity
Lack of friends in camp and fear of strangers
Having trouble with physical problems or physical handicaps
Not having as much spending money as some fellow campers
Being in camp against his will

How to treat the homesick patient:

Know the symptoms and be on the alert to catch the sufferer before it becomes acute and spreads.

Find a parent or friend substitute.

Keep him busy in appealing activities.

Do not ridicule or shame him; let him know this feeling is not uncommon.

If hysteria develops, ignore it. Do not let him call his parents by phone. Do not send word for parents to come after him. To leave camp prematurely because of homesickness does something undesirable to the child, who needs to be helped to conquer this fear.

BED-WETTING (ENURESIS)

This occurs in practically every camp. If a camper is a bed wetter, parents should note the fact on his information sheet, but some do not. Check should be made especially the first morning and the usual precautions taken thereafter.

EATING HABITS

Habits of eating that distress counselors may be: eating too fast, too much, too slowly (talking instead of eating), dislike of certain foods, and failure to eat desirable foods. Talks by the dining-room hostess, good example of the counselor, elimination of between-meal snacks, or counseling with the camp nurse or doctor in severe cases may lessen the problem.

ALLERGIES

Allergies are sometimes real and sometimes affected. The nurse should be aware of them and take appropriate measures to avoid distress.

THE CAMPER AS A GROUP MEMBER

Camping provides an unusually suitable setting for youngsters to develop in improved human relations. The camper needs to know that he is important as an individual, but he also needs to learn to live and work with others, finding his place in creative, democratic group-living situations. The camp affords these patterns:

Structured

The living unit—cabin mates and counselor, the smallest camp group.[3]
The activity unit ("discovery," "quest," "class")—a small group involved
  in activities planned by the camp or campers.
The complete camp unit—the larger camp fellowship.

Unstructured

Free-time groupings—special pals with whom one shares spontaneous activities.
Interest groups—those who share special interests without pre-planning
  by the camp.

Through his participation in these various groups, seeking to find
his place, accepting disciplines of group interaction, the camper
learns social values. The responsibility lies with the staff members
to help the campers make the most of these opportunities in group
living.

Those interested in a serious study of camp group work will find
several excellent books in this field. (See Bibliography at the end
of Part V.)

To provide for a more democratic camp, often a *camper council*
is organized, composed of representatives from each living group
or activity group. The council assists in camp planning according to
the ability of its members and according to the philosophy of the
camp.

LEADING THE CAMPER TO CHRIST

Evangelical camping is frankly evangelistic. It does not agree with
liberal church camping literature that states that no decision or
commitment to Christ should be sought at camp.

It is the work of the Holy Spirit to convict and convince of sin.
Camp provides an opportune setting for such a work of the Spirit—
while the camper and counselor talk quietly together in the out-of-
doors, or during the inspiration of a group worship experience.
Countless campers date their conversions to that high moment at

---

[3] ACA recommends a ratio of one adult counselor to every eight campers in
junior and junior high camps.

camp when they met Christ heart to heart in a definite, personal religious experience. That each camper might know Christ as Saviour and Friend is the ultimate aim of evangelical camping.

Each staff member should know how to lead a camper to Christ. He should be alert to take advantage of any opening which the Holy Spirit permits in dealing with campers about their souls, not being meddlesome or over-anxious, but alert to Spirit-directed opportunities.

Some evangelical camps place particular stress on counselor-oriented evangelism, with the counselor expected to deal personally with each camper sometime during the camp period. Other camps favor "mass" evangelistic methods, when an invitation is given during a public service. Probably most evangelical camps favor a combination of the two methods.

Caution must be exercised in the latter method that "high pressure" is not used, resulting in a mass response with little individual meaning. Much harm has been done by working on the impressionable minds of youth without a corresponding drawing of the Holy Spirit. But the fact that the method has been abused in some instances is no reason to abandon it. Public invitations may be given, emphasizing that individual commitment in an intelligent, meaningful act is desired. Care must be taken that every youth who responds to a public invitation receives the personal attention of a counselor.

But whether the opportunity comes in personal contact or public invitation, what should a counselor do to see the youth actually won to Christ? The counselor must be prepared in his own heart, sensitive to the leadings of the Holy Spirit in this most delicate work of linking the seeker's heart to the seeking heart of God. He should have a Bible in hand with marked passages, which are best memorized. A few are indicated below.

The *steps to salvation* are then explained:

Repent.   To be so sorry for our sins that we quit them. Luke 13:3.
Confess.   Name sins out to God, confessing them one by one, those which He brings to mind; agreeing to confess to man those wrongs which need making right. I John 1:9; Matt. 5:24.
Believe.   Christ died for our sins. I Cor. 15:3; Acts 16:31.
Ask.   Invite Christ to come in. Rev. 3:20; Matt. 7:7.

Accept. Salvation is a free gift, but it must be accepted. Eph. 2:8; John
11:12.

After Scripture for each of these steps is found and read by the
seeker, appropriate prayer should be made. The seeker himself
should pray, audibly if possible, with the counselor supplying words
as necessary. If these steps have been taken sincerely, God Himself
will give the assurance as faith reaches through to Him.

After the assurance of salvation is received, a prayer of thanksgiv-
ing is in order, or an appropriate chorus may be sung. The new
convert should witness at once to someone—publicly, if the conversion occurs in public, or to a close friend or counselor, if it is done
in private. The counselor should not leave the new convert without
giving some instruction in Christian living concerning Bible reading,
prayer, church attendance, help in temptation. This is an appropriate
time to give out nurture literature, such as *Being a Christian*, men-
tioned in "Follow-Up" in Part III.

What is more rewarding to any Christian than to be the instru-
ment of God in leading one of His children to Him? Every born-
again Christian should become adept in this vital work.

◈◈◈◈◈◈◈

15. THE CAMP STAFF

COUNSELING AND NON-COUNSELING

WHAT IS A COUNSELOR?

A camp director in charge of an extensive evangelical camping
program (ACA approved) gives his rule: "Teachers never counsel;
counselors never teach." Another director in a neighboring state is
just as emphatic: "Every camp staff member except the cook or
visiting missionary is in charge of a cabin." An evangelical youth

movement, whose camps are all ACA approved, has no camp pastor, expecting cabin counselors to do all evangelistic work.

Hence, within the framework of evangelical camping various definitions of a counselor may be found. In the larger sense a counselor is anyone in camp who deals directly with children, aside from the kitchen, maintenance, and business staff. In the stricter sense a counselor is the one in charge of a cabin of campers. For the purposes of this volume the word "counselor" is used in the former sense—counselors are all those concerned directly with the children.

STAFF RELATIONSHIPS

The charts in Part III show how the members of the camp staff interrelate in an organizational way. Yet when it comes to smoothly integrating the camp staff into a team, more is needed than a chart.

There are three usual divisions of the camp staff: administration, program, counseling. Administrative personnel usually have only casual relationship with the campers, program staff have more, and the cabin counselors have the most intimate contact.

Status strata should not be allowed to develop. Each staff member must feel that he is an important part of the team, whose ultimate aim is winning and nurturing the camper in Christ. Too, each must realize that his actions, attitudes, and even voice inflections have their place in demonstrating vital Christian living, or, unhappily, less than that. The scheduled classes in Bible study, the services, and the devotional periods, while important, will not be nearly as effective in teaching as will the life of each of the camp staff.

To be at their best spiritually, camp staff members, from handy boys to director, must take time for daily devotions, privately and in groups. To be at their best physically, they must take time for adequate rest and relaxation. The ACA recommendation is two hours off each day and twenty-four hours off every seven days.

STAFF MEETINGS

Camp staff meetings are of three types: planning, prayer and devotional, and training sessions.

The poorly planned camp with little or no pre-camp training will find a daily staff planning session a necessity. Too often there will be little time left for prayer or training because of the urgency in settling daily problems and orienting poorly trained staff members. Unfortunately these meetings too often, when pattern and morale are not established before camp, develop into contests of wills between those of conflicting opinions as to what should be done. Of course, this situation is neither desirable nor necessary. The remedy is obvious: pre-camp planning and staff training.

In the camp that has been carefully planned and that has a trained staff there will be little need for all-staff planning sessions. Then the daily staff meetings may become a time of prayer and spiritual fellowship, so necessary for attaining camp spiritual goals.

Some camps schedule daily staff meetings during the campers' free time, with a rotating skeleton staff on duty. Others have the meetings just after "lights out" at night for all except cabin counselors, who meet at another time. Some camps require administrative and program staff to meet an hour before campers' breakfast. Along with the morning meal, daily plans are discussed and settled, with plenty of time left for prayer. During the day counseling staff have their own prayer meetings; cooks and office staff take time for their own prayer hours. Prayer thus permeates the camp atmosphere.

A director of a year-around evangelical camping program states, "Such staff prayer sessions are not just 'nice'; they are an absolute necessity!" If eternal results are to be obtained from camping, they will do so in answer to prayer—of the staff, of parents, of home churches.

Training sessions for staff members (other than CITs) are being held in more church camps. Often these are regularly scheduled classes in camp theory and practice. More often they are informal sessions teaching special skills.

QUALIFICATIONS OF COUNSELORS

The following characteristics are desirable in camp counselors, though it is not expected that they will all be found in one individual. Some may be considered goals toward which to work. This listing may be made into a chart for self-evaluation by the counselor.

PHYSICAL

1. The ACA standard provides that a counselor should be at least 19 years of age.

2. He has health and physical stamina, a necessity to stand the rigors of day-long contact with children.

3. He has the ability to get up in the mornings.

4. He has a nervous system able to stand noise and the stress of living with children.

5. He knows his own physical limitations and is willing to abide by them, taking rest and relaxation as provided and necessary (at least two hours a day).

6. He has good health practices; he is neat in personal appearance.

SPIRITUAL (all-important in evangelical camping)

1. He is able to "share God" with the campers.

2. He walks close to Christ, engages in daily devotions.

3. He has the ability to show Christian attitudes under stress.

4. He accepts camping experience as a ministry, a service to Christ and His children.

5. He knows how to lead a camper to Christ; he is sensitive to the leadings of the Spirit in this work.

6. He is faithful in preparation of cabin devotions, Bible lessons, or other phases of religious activities in camp.

EMOTIONAL

1. He has a good degree of emotional maturity.

2. He realizes that campers' needs must come before personal pleasure. Camping is for the campers, not for the pleasure of the staff.

3. He strives to show equality to all, no favoritism.

4. He has objectivity in disciplinary situations, keeping from personal emotional involvement.

5. He is patient, poised in tense situations.

6. He has a sense of humor, can laugh at himself, is cheerful.

SOCIAL

1. He is outgoing, enjoys being with people.
2. He avoids spending time with staff that should be spent with campers; he is willing to give himself to the campers.
3. He is courteous to all.

ATTITUDES

1. He shows loyalty to the camp director, camp objectives, and other staff members.
2. He avoids criticism of others.
3. He is determined to enjoy camp and find the pleasant side even in a rainy day—or other disappointment.
4. He is democratic, not autocratic in position of authority.
5. He is able to cooperate and make adjustments.

SKILLS

1. He is willing to increase his knowledge of camping through study of books and attendance at training sessions.
2. He adds constantly to his resources: books, collections, pictures, etc.
3. He plans to excel in some field, learn new skills, improve older ones.
4. He enjoys living outdoors and is at home in it.
5. He knows how to impart enthusiasm to campers, stimulating them to better endeavor.

RECRUITING COUNSELORS

In too many one-week church camps, counselors are obtained by haphazard means, the director himself approaching camp not sure just who will "turn up" to help out on opening morning. With untrained staff, uninstructed in the goals and methods of the camp, the chances for effectiveness in the camp experience are greatly lessened.

If it is true that camps are only as successful as their counselors (it is), and if counselors need pre-camp training (they do), then better recruiting methods are indicated in many camps.

Lee Kingsley is director of Big Trout Lake Camp in Minnesota, a church camp that operates for three summer months serving various age groups, requiring nearly two hundred counselors per season. He presented these methods of recruiting at a CCA convention. They are used here by permission.

1. Appeal on the basis that the task is important, demanding one's best; not "we are desperate and need you."

2. Begin in the fall to recruit pastors, asking each to give one week during the summer, giving choice of date. Send second letter and others as needed until response is received. Pastors act as teachers only, not as counselors, and go home week ends.

3. A Counselor Prospect Sheet is mailed to pastors for giving names of prospects only; pastors are not to contact them; emphasize need for couples for coed camps.

4. Director writes to those whose names are given, sending a detailed Counselor Application Blank, which gives room for listing skills, education, experience, religious experience, health, references. The prospect is asked to pray about applying before filling out and returning the sheet.

5. From information on the blank and personal interview (if possible) the director hires his staff, not accepting all applicants. Those accepted receive mailings regarding staff policies, camp organization and control, assignment to specific duties.

6. All year long in publications, recruiting is highlighted. Appeal is made especially to men to give vacation time to camp. The number of counselors each church provides is given publicity each year. One-fourth of the promotion budget goes to recruiting staff.

7. Counselors, teachers, and some of the program staff are temporary, changing weekly as a new camp group moves in; permanent summer staff include administration, food services, some activity specialists, and maintenance.

8. Building a tradition of good counseling increases the flow of good counselors. At youth conventions, etc., training courses in camp counseling are scheduled.

The camp director who is responsible for a one-week church camp may adapt this plan to his own needs. The important aspect is to have a plan in recruiting that assures the staff's being hired early enough for them to enjoy benefits of pre-camp training.

ACA Camp Staff Application Blanks, 2¢ each, may be used as a guide in developing one's own. Evangelicals will wish to add space for spiritual qualifications and previous experience in church activities.

TRAINING THE STAFF

WHAT THEY SHOULD KNOW

By the time camp starts the counselor should have definite information about his particular camp as well as camping in general. This is a thoughtfully planned listing for a secular camp, pertinent also for evangelical camping:

IN GENERAL, training should help the counselor—

1. Know what a counselor does.
2. Gain some skill and knowledge in relation to his own job or interests.
3. Increase his understanding of the job of leadership of boys and girls in a camp situation, including importance of consideration for the individual camper.
4. Acquire (or review) skills in outdoor living, and acquaint him with other activities that are part of camp program.
5. Know something of "the camping way" and camping contribution to the total development of campers.
6. Understand general staff relationships and responsibilities.

SPECIFICALLY, for one camp, training should help the counselor—

1. Know the camp's particular situation, plan of action, ways of work:
   a. What the camp is like, its terrain and layout, it surrounding country, its neighbors.
   b. How the camp is organized; how programs are planned; the mechanics of camp living.
   c. The camp emphases or objectives; relation of these to the objectives of the sponsoring organization, if there is one.
   d. Equipment and facilities.
   e. History and traditions of the camp.
2. Know his own job:
   a. Job description; responsibilities for campers, to other staff, etc.
   b. Facilities and equipment for his use.

      c. Other staff members available to help him.
3. Feel secure in his job:
    a. Know arrangements:
        (1) Terms of employment, contracts, agreements.
        (2) Living arrangements.
        (3) Time off, and how it is arranged.
        (4) Equipment to be supplied by him; personal and otherwise.
        (5) Personal requirements, health certificate.
        (6) Financial arrangements.
        (7) Health, insurance, and other services available to him.
        (8) Arrangements for guests.
    b. Know who supervises him, and how it is to be done.
4. Know the relation of his job to total camp job:
    a. Know who other staff members are, what they do, and how he is expected to work with them.
5. Know routines for using facilities or equipment, or getting supplies.
6. Know the camper group—general background (social, economic, religious, cultural, geographic, etc.).
7. Know about records and reports:
    a. Those he will be expected to keep.
    b. Those he may be expected to use, or to which he will have access.
    c. Purpose and methods of making and keeping.
8. Know staff responsibilities, attitudes, limitations (if any):
    a. On the camp site.
    b. When off the camp, but in the vicinity.
    c. When away from camp with a camper group.
9. Have a chance to work with the whole staff, and with sections of the staff, to formulate objectives, ways of work, etc.[1]

STAFF MANUALS

All the information listed above for an individual camp forms the basis of the Staff Manual. This must be tailor-made for each camp. Some directors send the manual along with contract or notice of acceptance. Others prefer to give it out sheet by sheet during pre-camp training.

[1] Catherine T. Hammett, *A Camp Director Trains His Own Staff* (Martinsville, Ind.: American Camping Association, n.d.), pp. 10, 11.

CONTRACTS—JOB DESCRIPTIONS

All employed personnel should have contracts that clearly state the terms of employment. Each staff member should have a written job description listing all his duties in detail. These must be tailor-made from each camping organizational pattern. For a sample job description, see the one for camp directors in Part III.[2]

TRAINING TECHNIQUES

Before camp there are various methods that can be used to impart information needed by the counselors.

1. *Interviews* and *conferences* are desirable between director and counselors before camp.

2. Much can be done through *correspondence*. Information about camp policies, camp organization, contracts and agreements, and job descriptions, and the staff manual should be in the hands of the counselor before camp. Some camps distribute some of this material during pre-camp training.

3. *Pre-camp meetings* of staff off the camp site may accomplish much in getting the staff acquainted and oriented.

4. *Books* for reading before camp may be required, furnished by the camp committee.

5. *Attendance* at camp *workshops* and *conventions* (ACA, CCA, NSSA) is encouraged.

6. Completion of the *denominational leadership course* in camping (if there is one) should be expected of all staff before camp. This volume is designed as a text for such courses.

7. Each staff member should be encouraged to *take advantage of resources in the community* for developing skills: craft, swimming and lifesaving, nature, music, etc., according to abilities and interest of staff members. These are provided by Red Cross, YMCA, adult education courses, 4-H Club, etc.

PRE-CAMP ON-SITE TRAINING

The American Camping Association standards suggest three days

---

[2] *Church Camping for Junior Highs* and *Camping, Pioneer Girls Style* have good sections on job descriptions.

of on-site training preceding camp. This standard is applicable especially to long-term camping, but in church camping which must accomplish much in just a week (usually) only pre-camp training can assure a smooth-running camp.

These activities are suggested for such training:

Getting acquainted with the staff.
Planning by those staff members who will be working together.
Knowing the camp situation, plan of action.
Learning about the mechanics of camp living.
Learning, practicing, and reviewing camping skills.
Learning about the campers, especially those to be in the counselor's care.
Settling into own living quarters.
Preparing the camp staff spiritually; devotional talks, prayer times together, discussion of spiritual goals of the camp, instruction in how to lead a camper to Christ, familiarizing all camp staff with the pattern of Bible class curriculum.

Many church camps of one week's duration have not yet reached the point of requiring three days' training. The following outline is the program of a one-day on-site training period, a first attempt by Warm Beach Camp in western Washington, a conference-type, church camping program. Following this session leaders agreed that, while it had been helpful, a longer period was needed to accomplish all that they desired.

Morning Sessions
  9:00 Devotions
  9:15 Orientation of Camp Program—Representative of Sponsoring Body
10:00 Camp Bible Curriculum—Program Director
        Orientation of CITs—Camp Director and Head Counselors
10:30 Hug the Mug
10:45 The Camp Counselor—Head Counselor
11:15 Smell the Flowers
12:00 Follow Your Nose

Afternoon Sessions
  1:00 Use of Camp Facilities—Camp Committee Member
        Insurance: Liability—Camp Director
        Mental and Physical Well-Being—Nurse

1:30 Understanding the Junior High Camper—Public School Teacher
2:00 Our "Club" Program—Program Director
2:30 Our Craft Program—Craft Director
3:00 Make a Break
3:30 Understanding the Junior Camper—College Professor
4:00 Some Aspects of Effective Counseling—Head Counselor
4:30 Tour of the Camp Facilities (Or have you had enuf?)
5:30 Scrape the Kettle.

Is attendance compulsory? Some camp directors state flatly that non-attendance at pre-camp training automatically means dismissal. Paid employees can be handled more strictly than volunteers in this matter. In any case when this training is provided, staff members (even experienced ones) must recognize that it is essential.

Methods in pre-camp training include:

1. Talks and lectures—most efficient way to present much material, least efficient as an actual learning experience.
2. Discussions—unless carefully guided, these can waste time, but they do stimulate thinking.
3. Demonstrations of techniques—valuable, superior to verbal explanation.
4. Practice by staff of actual techniques—assures learning especially in field of campcraft or recreational skills.
5. Role playing—used profitably. Example: Two persons take parts of homesick camper and counselor. More benefit is derived when not just two persons do this, others watching, but the whole group is divided into two-person teams, each assuming a role. After five noisy minutes, each team reports on progress.
6. Use of visual aids: posters, films, slides, exhibits, etc.
7. Use of publications, reference books, resource material, on hand to exhibit during training sessions.
8. Observation of regular activities (not just planned demonstrations).

ACCREDITED CAMPING COURSES

While probably the majority of evangelical colleges, Bible schools, and seminaries have yet to include camping courses in their curricula, several forward-looking institutions are doing noteworthy work in this field. In use are these patterns: academic courses in schools with no field work, or with subsequent field work in approved camps; school-directed courses on the camp site with concurrent or subsequent field work; camp-directed instruction and field work recognized by schools with no direct affiliation with the camp. Some conservative schools offering credit in camping according to these patterns are: Moody Bible Institute, Taylor University, Wheaton, Bethel, Seattle Pacific, Carson-Newman, Cedarville, Evangel, Grace, Goshen, Westmont, Trinity, Calvary Bible colleges. Some give credit in Christian education, others in physical education.

Southwest Baptist, Western Evangelical, Southern Baptist, Dallas, Bethel, and Trinity are among seminaries giving graduate credits for camping courses in Christian education.

NSSA Camp Commission and CCA are encouraging schools and camps to institute such mutually beneficial training programs.

COUNSELOR-IN-TRAINING PROGRAM (CIT)

Since it is obvious that camp success depends upon trained counselors, camp leaders came to the logical conclusion that they themselves must do more about training future staff members. The CIT program sprang into existence during the last war especially in YMCA camps.

CITs are sometimes known as LITs (Leaders in Training) or LEAs (from Leaders). CITs are older campers, usually sophomores or juniors in high school, enrolled for leadership training in camp. In some youth camps they are used with other campers the same age, a special incentive to hold able campers. In other cases CITs are used only in junior camps, in the belief that in junior high camps the age is too close, and that frictions arise over this specially privileged group. Usually the CIT in a junior camp pays nothing and receives no salary. In youth camps he may receive free or half tuition.

This program for a two-year training of CITs is recommended for a term camp of eight weeks' duration:

During the first year:

A satisfying group experience with one's peers.
  (CITs live, work, and play together as a cabin group.)

A broadening of camping skills.
(Each CIT receives instruction in his weaker skills.)
A successful work experience.
(Each CIT is rotated on several individual or group tasks.)
A self-appraisal and improvement program.
(CITs participate in reading, discussion, and practice of leadership skills.)

And during the second year:

Self-appraisal and improvement—Continued.
(Each individual works on his own leadership needs.)
Theory and practice of leadership—Continued.
(Further reading, discussion, and practice at a greater depth.)
Practical experience in cabin leadership.
(CIT lives with a cabin group to observe and assist the counselor.)
Practical experience in program leadership.
(CIT is assigned to his strong program activity to observe and assist the leader with instruction and supervision.)[3]

Where there are CITs, there must be special regulations regarding time off, use of camp facilities when not used by campers, later bedtimes, provision for special social activities, snacks. These regulations should be written out and sent to the CIT along with his application, which must be signed by parents before he is accepted for training. CITs should participate in pre-camp training sessions. Evaluation sheets are to be filled out by the CIT director or counselor with whom each CIT serves. A self-evaluation sheet for the trainee is also valuable.

The major purpose of a CIT program is to give training. Other purposes are to provide assistance in maintenance (a few hours a day) and to give counselors more free time. When this program is adapted to one-week church camping, the training must necessarily be briefer. In such camps that operate throughout the summer, the CIT is asked to remain from week to week if his performance is acceptable.

[3] Eugene A. Turner, Jr., *The CIT in Residence Camping* (New York: Association Press, 1961), p. 37.

BIBLIOGRAPHY

The following books for further study of campers and camp staff are arranged under each heading in recommended order of purchase for the average evangelical camp. See bibliographies listed in Appendix for further related publications.

UNDERSTANDING THE CAMPERS

Soderholm, Marjorie Elaine. *Understanding the Pupil:* Part II, *The Primary and Junior Child,* and Part III, *The Adolescent.* Grand Rapids: Baker Book House, 1958. $1.25 each. (Evangelical in emphasis.)
Hartwig, Marie, and Myers, Bettye. *Children Are Human (Even at Camp)* ⸱and *Children Are Human (If the Counselors Really Know Them).* Minneapolis: Burgess Publishing Company, 1961, 1962. $2.25 each.
Moser, Clarence G. *Understanding Boys* and *Understanding Girls.* New York: Association Press, 1953, 1957. $3.50 each.
Children's Bureau Publications. *The Adolescent in Your Family* and *Your Child From Six to Twelve.* Washington: Government Printing Office, 1955, 1949. 25¢, each.

CHILD EVANGELISM

Coleman, Frank G. *The Romance of Winning Children.* Cleveland: Union Gospel Press, 1948. $2.00. (Evangelical in emphasis.)
Overholtzer, J. Irvin. *A Handbook on Child Evangelism.* Grand Rapids: International Child Evangelism Fellowship, 1955. 60¢ (Evangelical in emphasis.)
Dobbins, Gaines S. *Winning the Children.* Nashville: Broadman Press, 1953. $2.00. (Evangelical in emphasis.)

CAMPER AS A GROUP MEMBER

Camper Guidance. Martinsville, Ind.: American Camping Association, 1961. 75¢.
Coyle, Grace Longwell. *Group Work with American Youth.* Harper and Row. $4.00.

TRAINING THE STAFF

Hammett, Catherine T. *A Camp Director Trains His Own Staff.* Martinsville, Ind.: American Camping Association, 1945. 50¢.

Camp Administrative Forms and Suggested Procedures in the Area of Personnel. Martinsville, Ind.: American Camping Association. 50¢.

Hartwig, Marie. *Workbook for Camp Counselor Training.* Minneapolis: Burgess Publishing Company, 1960. $4.00.

Turner, Eugene A., Jr. *The CIT in Residence Camping.* New York: Association Press, 1961. $1.25.

CIT Guide. Martinsville, Ind.: American Camping Association. 1963. $1.00.

CAMP COUNSELING

Mattson, Lloyd D. *Camping Guideposts.* Chicago: Moody Press, 1963. $2.50. (Evangelical in emphasis.)

MacKay, Joy. *Creative Counseling for Christian Camp.* Scripture Press, 1966. $1.50.

How to Be a Camp Counselor. Wheaton, Ill.: Scripture Press, 1959. 75¢. (Evangelical in emphasis.)

Ledlie, John H., and Holbein, F. W. *Camp Counselor's Manual.* New York: Association Press, 1958. $1.25.

Doty, Richard. *The Character Dimension of Camping.* Association Press, 1960. $4.75.

Doherty, Kenneth. *Solving Camp Behavior Problems.* New York: Association Press, 1940. $1.00.

Mitchell, Viola, and Crawford, Ida. *Camp Counseling.* Philadelphia: W. B. Saunders Company, 1961. $6.25.

STUDY HELPS

1. What must the camp counselor learn about his campers?
2. Describe how God and His Church can provide for the eight basic needs of children.
3. What is the religious approach (not psychological) in dealing with behavior problems?
4. What do you consider the maximum number of campers that a cabin counselor should have in his living unit in a junior camp? A junior high camp?
5. What are principles to be observed in leading a child to Christ?

6. What is your definition of a camp counselor?
7. What are the most important characteristics of a camp counselor?
8. What is the most important aspect of recruiting counselors?
9. What should a staff manual contain?
10. Name ways a camp director may train his staff before pre-camp on-site training.
11. What are the purposes of a CIT program?

PROJECTS

1. Design a camp counselor application blank.
2. Outline a program for a three-day, on-site, pre-camp training period.

VI. HOW TO DO IT

PROGRAM

CAN CAMPING'S WORTH BE MEASURED?

"Where lies the magic of camping? Truly there is no single answer. It can be different things to different campers. But it weaves a strong spell. It is the little things, half remembered but never wholly forgotten, that come flooding back in future years at the glint of sunlight on still water, the scent of pine forest or woodsmoke, the endless, eternal canopy of night stars. It is the undying heritage of childhood that never fully leaves an adult.

"There are some who would measure the worth of a camp by the extent of its buildings, the monetary value of its equipment, or the cost of its operation. But, the true values of a camp are not for sale. Can anyone buy pride in accomplishment, close friendship, or joy?

"There can be no words to catch the spell of camping; no formula to bring its magic within the grasp of the unknowing. It is part of the American heritage, from the days when buffalo ran wild and our Red Brothers were masters of the woods and streams. Deep in the heart of every child lies the precious spirit of adventure, and it is the warmth of this spirit that grows with camping.

"Who can measure the silence of the deep woods, the peace of the out-of-doors, the spirit of brotherhood that dwells in such surroundings? Can one hope to recapture that priceless moment, when, sleeping under countless stars, one feels the nearness to Things Eternal and catches a fleeting glimpse of the true power and majesty of God?

"The American Indian felt its power and knew its majesty. We but pass on his ideals to others. In the words of the poet:

> Ye who love the haunts of nature
> Love the sunshine in the meadow
> Love the wind among the branches,
> Love the shadow of the forest,
> And the rain shower and the snow storm,
> And the rushing of the rivers.
>
> Ye, whose hearts are fresh and simple
> Who have faith in God and Nature
> That the feeble hands and helpless
> Groping blindly in the darkness
> Touch God's Right Hand in the darkness
> And are lifted up and strengthened.

"May we follow in the footprints of their moccasins." [1]

[1] Charles R. Jenkins, in Kenneth Webb (editor), *Light from a Thousand Campfires* (New York: Association Press, 1960), pp. 365, 366.

〰〰〰〰〰〰〰
16. PROGRAM PLANNING

TYPES OF PROGRAMS

There are two major ideological battlegrounds in camping—philosophy and program. These are interrelated, for philosophy is the foundation upon which the superstructure of program should be built.

Camp program is often defined as everything that happens at camp, both spontaneous and planned. In the part that results from planning there are basic similarities in any camp—three meals a day, rest and sleeping. But from here camps take off in all directions, each making its own path in the tangled but enchanted field which is camping. There needs to be tolerance at this point. What is adequate for one should not be despised by another. Each program pattern may have verities for its own constituents.

These are the two extreme types of programs (refer to pragmatic camp vs. evangelical camp in Part II):

DECENTRALIZED, UNSTRUCTURED, COUNSELOR AND SMALL-GROUP CENTERED

All activities are selected by the campers; small groups are led by the counselors at a time and pace desired by the group. There are no scheduled activities. Such camps major in individual attention to campers and require well-trained counselors able alone to lead the camper into desirable camping experiences. If they fail, the camper suffers.

CENTRALIZED, ACTIVITY-CENTERED, CONFERENCE TYPE

Activities are scheduled, and the entire camp is expected to participate at times and places designated. Activity specialists lead their segments of the program; counselors have care of campers only at the cabin. Such camps can give little regard to individual needs but may use less-trained staff.

These two extremes and modifications give the following classifications:

1. Totally unstructured program.
2. Skeletal structuring: meals, bedtime, rising.
3. Partially scheduled; skeletal plus a few scheduled activities.
4. Scheduled, with choice of activities by campers.
5. Scheduled, without camper choice.

Numbers 3 and 4 provide the "in between" group which probably takes in the majority of present-day evangelical camps. These are often called modified decentralized or conference type with camper choice. They can give attention to the individual, yet if a staff member is ineffective, his weakness does not affect so seriously the whole camp experience of the camper. Less-trained personnel may be used in some positions. The camper receives the advantage of close contact with several of the camp staff.

"Primitive" camping is entering evangelical circles. This seeks to avoid elements in the camp program that can be included just as well on the city playground; it concentrates on outdoor skills, hiking, woodsmanship, canoe tripping, etc. "Primitive" camping is usually found more in decentralized programs than in conference types.

TO BE CONSIDERED IN PROGRAM PLANNING

FACTORS

The following are the factors that any camp committee must keep in mind in program planning for a particular camp:

1. Camper group: age, number, sex, experience, health needs, interests.
2. Staff: number, qualifications, interests.
3. Camp situation: i.e., equipment, topography, set-up, finances.
4. Weather, climate.
5. Philosophy of sponsoring organization or individuals.
6. Camp traditions and emphasis.
7. Parent expectations.
8. Length of sessions.
9. Structure.
   a. Time-wise (scheduled vs. unscheduled).
   b. Group-wise (individual, cabin, intra-cabin, total camp).[1]

---

[1] *Camp Administration Course Outline* (Martinsville, Ind.: American Camping Association, 1961), p. 11.

These are underlying principles to be considered:

1. The tempo of the camp must not be hectic. Fatigue in camp is a subject about which much is written in camping literature. Probably most camps attempt too much for the physical good of the camper. This is especially true in short-term church camping. It is better to add more days to camp than to crowd the schedule.

2. Activities should be balanced: active vs. quiet; small group vs. entire camp fellowship; intellectual vs. physical.

3. There should be sufficient free time to allow the camper individual pursuits—just to live and to do what he wants to.

4. The camp program must allow for flexibility to meet changing situations and needs of the campers.

5. Grading of activities in camps with programs for varying ages is essential. An over-all bland program is to be avoided. Some activities should be kept distinctive for the next age group. (Example: Junior ages do not have leathercraft, do not go out on overnight hikes. These are reserved for junior high ages. Canoe tripping is reserved for senior highs.)

6. The program should allow for motivation of campers.

7. Included should be only those activities for which adequate safety measures may be provided as outlined in ACA program safety standards.

AWARDS AND COMPETITION (CAMPER MOTIVATION)

Early camps were highly competitive, with the camp divided into groups that battled it out for points throughout camp. Traces of this competition remain in some camps where some counselors are still bogged down in complicated keeping of daily records.

Competition in life is inevitable. Whether it deserves prominence in camp is a question that has divided camp leaders for many years. Those who have discontinued it state happily that they like camping much better without the intense rivalry and pressure to excel.

Individual awards do stimulate better performance. While this perhaps should not be true, there are too few youth leaders who can motivate learning for its own intrinsic value. Public education finds it essential to give grades and awards to stimulate students, threatening poorer ones with failure. The danger of giving awards in camping (and grades in school) is that the youth achieves for the sake of the award rather than the joy of learning or doing.

Scouting and religious youth programs find camp an opportune time for members to pass requirements for badges. Certainly those who meet standards of excellence in camp activities (swimming, lifesaving, riflery, etc.) should receive recognition from such national organizations, as the National Rifle Association, Camp Archery Association, American Red Cross, Audubon Society, etc. The giving of good-camper certificates, etc., may set goals for campers. These thus serve a purpose, as long as they can be given fairly without complicated record keeping, daily checking of points, and the like, which take the joy out of life for counselor and camper alike. A desirable emphasis is for the camper to compete with his own record, doing his best rather than competing with records of others.

CAMP SCHEDULES

There is no "correct" daily schedule for a camp. Schedules depend entirely on local camp conditions. The ones presented here are typical of the modified decentralized and conference type camps.

JUNIOR CAMPS

Modified Decentralized

7:30 Reveille
8:00 Breakfast
8:30 Cabin cleanup and private devotions
9:15 Small-group activities to be decided by group
11:45 Ready for dinner
12:00 Dinner
1:00 Rest hour
2:00 Small-group activities including swimming

Conference Type with Camper Choice

7:30 Reveille
8:00 Breakfast
8:30 Cabin cleanup and private devotions
9:15 Bible class
10:30 Special activities under activity specialists (choice)
11:45 Ready for dinner
12:00 Dinner
1:00 Rest hour
2:00 Special activities (choice)

4:45 Free time	3:00 Recreation including swimming
5:30 Supper	5:00 Prepare for supper
6:00 Free time	5:30 Supper
6:45 Campfire, often small group	6:00 Free time
7:45 Talks with counselor, prepare for bed, cabin devotions	7:00 All-camp evening vespers
8:30 Taps	8:00 Prepare for bed, cabin devotions
	9:00 Taps

JUNIOR HIGH CAMP

7:00 Reveille	7:00 Reveille
7:30 Private devotions	7:30 Flag raising
7:45 Breakfast	7:45 Breakfast
8:15 Cabin cleanup	8:15 Cabin cleanup and private devotions
9:00 Small-group activity	9:00 Morning chapel
11:45 Prepare for dinner	9:30 Bible class
12:00 Dinner	10:15 Special activities (choice)
1:00 Rest hour	11:45 Prepare for dinner
2:00 Special-interest groups	12:00 Dinner
3:00 Recreation and work projects	1:00 Rest hour
5:00 Free time	2:00 Special activities (choice)
5:30 Supper	3:00 Recreation
6:00 Recreation	5:00 Free time or variety hour
7:00 Evening program ending with campfire (usually small group)	5:30 Supper
	6:00 Free time
8:45 Prepare for bed, cabin devotions	7:00 All-camp evening vespers
	8:15 Campfire
9:30 Taps	8:45 Prepare for bed, cabin devotions
	9:30 Taps

17. PROGRAM ELEMENTS

Since there exist so many excellent helps in specific program elements and because the purpose of this volume is to present only a survey of camping, this section does not give specific techniques. It is a brief treatment of program elements. Further helps are suggested in the Bibliography at the end of Part VI.

THOSE MEETING PHYSICAL NEEDS

MEALS

Breakfast is often served cafeteria style, which permits a more leisurely beginning of the day.

Dinner, the heaviest meal of the day, is suggested by many camping authorities as most appropriate at noon to meet the needs of campers for more food energy for afternoon activities and for the convenience of the cooks.

Supper, a simpler meal, is often followed by song time. The evening meal is a favored time for cookouts by small groups.

REST HOUR

After the noon meal is the recommended time for rest. Some state laws require an hour period with camper prone on his bunk. Some quiet activities may be permitted, such as reading, letter writing, Scripture memorization. If campers seem fatigued toward the end of camp, rest hour may be increased.

RISING AND RETIRING

Recommended sleep period for juniors is 10 to 10½ hours per night; for junior highs, 9½ to 10. In junior camps especially, quiet activities should precede bedtime.

DRESSING, WASHING, BATHING

Junior girls will require help in dressing and fixing hair. Junior boys and often junior high boys need supervision to see that they change into clean clothes instead of wearing the same tee shirts and underclothing all week. They will need reminders in personal cleanliness, brushing teeth, taking hot-water baths, etc. Daily swims are not sufficient.

CABIN HOUSEKEEPING

Before breakfast or just after are favored times for cabin cleanup. Daily cabin inspection is common, with all cabins passing given some type of recognition. Choosing the "cleanest cabin" often resolves itself into a matter of personal opinion (or prejudice) of the inspector, though many camps give awards therefor. A Cabin Housekeeping Check Sheet left daily in the cabin by the inspector will help campers to know the basis of any grading.

HEALTH HABITS

The counselor checks on the health habits and condition of his charges daily, watching for symptoms of illness. The camp nurse will check daily with counselors.

RELIGIOUS ACTIVITIES

Every phase of the camp program should make its contribution to the total spiritual impact of camp. But in evangelical camping scheduled activities will accentuate this.

CAMP CURRICULUM FOR CHRISTIAN LIVING

Although decentralized camping does not use planned courses, in conference-type camps they are considered essential. Several denominational and independent publishers are offering camp curriculum series, which are improving in quality as publishers better understand camping philosophy. They offer a decided improvement over having each counselor prepare his own Bible study materials. Most have a teacher's manual and a pupil's workbook or looseleaf "Log Book," to which other materials of the individual camp may be added. Often the camp curriculum provides, besides Bible study, the theme for the one-week camp, with a daily program of nature exploration, cabin devotions, etc.

DEVOTIONS

Private devotions should be encouraged for each camper, with a time scheduled when he may be alone with his Bible.

Cabin devotions are the spiritual highlight of the day for the cabin counselor. This is the time he shares with his campers spiritual truths that are meaningful to him. They should be carefully planned in prayer and apropos to his own group. Just before bedtime is a preferred time, though sometimes devotions are held after breakfast or before rest hour.

CAMPER PRAYER MEETINGS

Attendance is always voluntary at camp prayer meetings. Often these are organized spontaneously by the campers themselves after public encouragement.

MORNING CHAPEL

Held outdoors if possible, morning chapel features a devotional talk on Christian living by one of the counselors, a visiting missionary, or other guest speaker. This is a good time for public testimonies by campers. Decentralized camping avoids such daily, all-camp meetings, feeling that more may be accomplished in small groups.

EVENING VESPERS—CAMPFIRE

In conference-type camps evening vespers are devotional meetings usually held in the chapel, with Scripture reading, prayers, special music, and a speaker. (If mass evangelism is used, this is the time for it.) The meeting may be a Galilean service at the lake front, a communion service, or a fagot fire consecration service.

Some groups begin with a secular emphasis around a campfire, tending toward a religious close. Others begin with the religious service in the chapel, then dismiss this for a secular gathering around a campfire later.

Campfires add much to camp and are easily provided. One should be scheduled at the slightest opportunity. Somebody has said, "We are all arsonists at heart, finding nothing more thrilling than a camp-fire."

In decentralized camping such all-camp groups are discouraged except in rare cases. In liberal church camping the evening gathering does not necessarily have a religious emphasis.

MEALTIME GRACES

Saying of graces is a novelty to many campers. They need to learn the beauty of this practice. Grace should not be said in a prefunctory manner. Some camps have different cabins in charge at different meals. Some have "family worship" right after breakfast with the group still around the tables.

NATURE IN CAMP

There are three usual approaches to nature in camp:

1. It is ignored. Campers and staff are so intent on carrying out their schedules that they do not have time to watch the ants at work, the bird half-hidden in the leafy branch, the stars that hang so low at night. In such camps, the site may as well be the civic auditorium where things of nature would not bother the smooth operation of the program.

2. There is formal nature study in classes under a nature counselor. This is an improvement as long as the "study" part does not remove the joy and wonder to be found in nature discoveries; as long as fulfilling requirements of the course does not become the goal.

3. Nature permeates the camp program. This is the best atmosphere for nature education. Every counselor, no matter how uninformed, is learning along with his campers to enjoy nature more. Each staff member strives to stimulate the curiosity of the campers, leading to further self-discoveries. There may be a nature counselor, who is the resource person, knowing more answers than most, but who wisely leads the camper to find his own answers in reference books or by further observation.

Aids to nature study may take the following forms:

Nature hikes are leisurely jaunts for opening the senses to God's creations, just for the joy of seeing, hearing, tasting, touching, feeling the wonders of the out-of-doors: rocks, flowers, birds, insects, trees, shrubs, leaves of a hundred designs, sky, clouds, grass, wildlife, soil, water. Such a hike should teach *awareness* to those things that usually are passed by without notice.

A nature trail can be part of even the smallest camp site. Signs made in the craft shop remind the passer-by of interesting specimens, formations, or viewpoints.

A nature museum can be placed near the entrance to the nature trail in a shelter. It is a display area of gathered treasures: a list of birds identified on the site with date seen, living specimens, collections. Possibilities are limited only by imagination of the campers.

Reference books are indispensable for identifying and labeling specimens.

Audubon camp materials provide a planned program with many variations that have been used in camps to good advantage. Order the descriptive leaflet. (See address in Appendix.)

Conservation practices should be taught along with nature appreciation. Campers should learn that looking at and then leaving wildflowers is good practice. Ask them to consider what would happen if one hundred campers for eight weeks in summer each cut one green branch for roasting marshmallows. An ACA publication, *You and Conservation, A Check List for Counselors,* 10¢ each, should be in the hands of each camp staff member.

Nature crafts can teach children to make camp souvenirs from materials native to the camp site or elsewhere. These include shells, cones, reeds and rushes, pine needles, cornstalks, bark, branches for whittling, fungi, native clays, native paints and juices, etc., from which evolve bone craft, nut craft, leaf prints, collages, limb plaques, seed craft, dried bouquets, feather craft, gourd craft, horn craft, etc.

THE ARTS

MUSIC

It is a moment long remembered. Slowly behind the towering pines sinks the golden sun, reflected in the gleaming ripples on the lake. From the lips of worshiping campers almost spontaneously come the words:

> Holy, holy, holy, Lord God of Hosts
> Heaven and earth are full of Thee
> Heaven and earth are praising Thee
> O Lord, most high.

Music is the language of the soul, and in camp, music should be as natural as breath: trail songs on the way to the waterfront; nonsense camping songs in cabins and around the campfire; hymns for the sacred, solemn moments; religious choruses for gayer times; anybody's favorite (barring the latest hit tunes) around the supper table.

Christian camps may add much to their atmosphere by more singing. The ACA songbook, *SING!*, 50¢, as well as standard hymnbooks should be part of every counselor's equipment. The music counselor plans music for group gatherings, may train a chorus in conference-type camps, arranges informal musical groups. Musical instruments at camp — accordions, banjos, ukeleles, guitars, cornets, trumpets, etc. — are allowed at the discretion of the camp committee. Radios are taboo in cabins.

ART

Pencils for sketching, charcoal, oils, pastels, ink, all offer mediums for budding camp artists. Perfection rarely results, but this is an expressive activity that more church camps are using.

WRITING

Journalism should be restricted to older children. In junior camps any camp paper must be published by the camp staff. In junior high camps campers may write and publish under supervision.

Poetry and stories of surprisingly good quality have been written by junior high ages in camp. In church camping more opportunities for creative writing could profitably be provided.

DRAMA

In junior high camps skits around the campfire are fun. Few youth at this age are writers of drama, but they do like to be in a production. Bible dramatizations planned by the campers themselves stimulate creativity. Short-term camping offers little time for dramatic productions.

STORYTELLING

Done by counselors during rest hour or other free time, or by campers themselves, this activity adds much to camp life.

CAMPCRAFTS

Instead of commercial crafts or organized sports, which are so common in the everyday life of modern youth, many camps are returning to campcrafts as more appropriate camp programming. These are activities that fire the imagination of youth. No food tastes so good as that one cooks oneself over his buddy burner or campfire. What is better fun for the youngster than being out in the field with bobbing compass needle pointing the way back to camp, as he sharpens his skill in the fine art of orienteering? To boys of another generation, who daily chopped wood for the kitchen range, an ax meant work. But to today's youth an ax biting into a log recalls the romance of frontier days. Every camp that has limited itself to standard activities which could be carried on just as well in the church basement or city playground needs to open its heart and mind to the possibilities in campcrafts.

The field of campcrafts has been classified by the American Camping Association into ten areas. The Association has set up a training program with three degrees in this field, giving ratings for Campcrafters, Advanced Campcrafters, and Trip Crafters upon completion of increasingly difficult training courses. The courses are presented in various parts of the nation and comprise valuable training for church camp counselors. Candidates must be 18 years of age to take this training. The text is *Your Own Book of Campcraft* by Catherine Hammett, a Cardinal pocket book, available on newsstands (50¢) or purchasable in quantity from ACA at a discount to camps for resale. Each camper will enjoy having his own text.

Since the requirements of the first rating are near the level that could be used in junior and junior high campcraft programs, the ten requirements are listed here. These can and do form the basis of campcrafting in some evangelical camps.

REQUIREMENTS FOR CERTIFICATE IN ACA CAMPCRAFT
TRAINING PROGAM

Firecraft

Demonstrate ability to:
(a) select and prepare a firesite.
(b) select and store supply of natural materials for tinder, kindling, and fuel for a one meal fire.
(c) build and use a fire for simple cooking.
(d) extinguish fire and prepare firesite for leaving.
List safety and conservation practices observed.

Food (Cookouts)

Plan, prepare, and pack a balanced trail lunch requiring no cooking.
Share in setting up a simple trail cookout site.
Plan, pack, and prepare a well-balanced meal, demonstrating three types of simple outdoor cooking.
Demonstrate clean-up techniques, including dishwashing and disposal of rubbish and waste water.
[Each camper should have at some time during the camping season, even in conference-type camps, the experience of preparing at least one meal in the open—not just the "camp picnic" or roasting wieners. Cookouts and campouts must be cleared with program director and kitchen staff with 24 hours' notice. They are best carried on in small groups. Camp program and campcraft books give methods and menus.]

Toolcraft

Demonstrate ability to handle, care for, and store pocketknife, ax, bow, or buck saw.
Make and use a piece of simple camp equipment, using some of these tools.

Ropecraft

Know various types of rope and demonstrate proper care of rope. Demonstrate ability to:
(a) whip a rope.
(b) tie and use one each of the following knots: joining, stopper, loop, end-securing.
Demonstrate ability to make three types of lashing and make a simple lashed article.

Gear and Shelter

Demonstrate selection, packing, and carrying of personal gear suitable for locality, including clothing, program, and safety items for a one-day trip.

Share in selecting, packing, and carrying group gear for a one-day trip.

Make an item of individual gear.

Map and Compass [Orienteering]

Demonstrate ability to read a compass by giving bearings to designated objects.

Demonstrate ability to give direction by the sun and by the stars.

Demonstrate ability to give and follow simple directions, using sketch map, trail signs, etc.

Health and Safety

State ten health and safety practices in relation to campcraft activities.

Demonstrate use of good health and safety practices in all parts of this test.

Outline preventive measures and first aid procedures for simple emergencies in hiking and campcrafting.

Nature and Conservation

Demonstrate conservation practices in all parts of this test.

Be able to identify three common native woody plants used in any part of this test.

Be able to identify three poisonous or harmful plants or animals found in locality, and know precautions of treatment for same.

Indicate five good or poor conservation practices in immediate camp or trip area.

Trips

In a group of not more than ten, share in planning for, carrying out, and evaluating a day trip away from the living area; include one meal with two types of outdoor cooking; demonstrate practice of personal hygiene and camp sanitation.

Leadership

Work out a plan for helping campers to acquire similar skills including camper-participation in planning and carrying out a day's trip.[1]

RECREATION

WATERFRONT

Swimming is the most universally liked activity in camping. That hazards are involved is acknowledged. Hence the camp will carefully plan its waterfront program according to approved safety standards (ACA, YWCA, YMCA, and American Red Cross). These include buddy system, time in water, checking-out system, marked swimming areas, lifesaving equipment, trained personnel.

Many children go to camp to learn to swim; hence teaching campers to swim should be a goal of every camp. The Red Cross Water Safety Ladder should be used, which provides awards and certificates for each of these: Beginner in Swimming, Advanced Beginner, Intermediate Swimmer, Swimmer, Junior Life Saving.

All these are open to junior and junior high youth. Opportunity for passing each test should be given at camp. Other courses which may be profitably taken by older campers and counselors allow them to achieve the rating of Advanced Swimmer, Water Safety Aide, or Water Safety Instructor. The latter rating (WSI) should be held by every waterfront counselor.

BOATING

The boating counselor should follow all safety regulations as approved by the American Red Cross, whose Ladder to Smallcraft Safety provides certificates in Basic Boating, Canoeing, and Sailing.

American Red Cross Aquatic and Small Craft Schools are conducted throughout the nation every year. Camps often pay tuition of their waterfront personnel to these schools. Local American Red Cross offices can give date and location of such schools.

---

[1] *Campcraft Certification Program* (Martinsville, Ind.: American Camping Association, 1962), 10¢.

SPORTS

Organized sports, such as volleyball and baseball, are no longer encouraged by many camping authorities. With the emphasis in the program on activities that can best be done at camp, these games associated with city life, gymnasiums, and playgrounds are not considered necessary. This does not mean that an occasional ball game is prohibited. But daily ones as held in some camps do indicate a poverty of ideas on the part of the camp program director and a lack of understanding as to what constitutes camping.

Some junior high camps carry on tournaments in shuffleboard, horseshoe pitching, ping-pong, handball, tennis, etc. Whether this constitutes good camping practice must be decided by the camp committee on the basis of its philosophy.

FREE TIME

Camp should allow sufficient time for the camper to follow individual pursuits, just to live, to dream, to wander about with pals, to play informally, to do just what he wants to. This, too, is important in camp. For the unimaginative, a listing of "What to do in free time" may be posted. Scheduling excessive free time should not become a way for camp personnel to escape responsibility.

GAMES

Every cabin counselor should come to camp with a store of tricks, puzzles, and games, played with simple or no equipment. (Example: A hilarious one such as Lemmy Sticks [2] will spread like wildfire through camp—and also provide a craft project in making the sticks.)

The recreational director will be prepared with games for large groups which provide much fun. Instructions for these are easily obtained.

[2] See Catherine Hammett and Virginia Musselman, *The Camp Program Book* (New York: Association Press, 1951), p. 166.

HIKING

Hiking just for the fun of getting somewhere is still a joy of camping. It differs from nature hiking or other special-purpose jaunts.

ARCHERY

Long-term camps often offer bow and arrow making in their craft programs. Short-term camps usually do not have time for this, but both will find archery a popular sport. Camps should affiliate with the Camp Archery Association, following its achievement and safety programs.

RIFLERY

Both boys and girls like riflery. A rifle range constructed and conducted according to approved safety regulations adds much interest to the camp program. Awards and medals from the National Rifle Association will give motivation to the program. The instructor should hold an instructor's rank in this organization.

FISHING

Happy is the camp that has good fishing on its site or nearby. All state regulations should be observed. The fishing counselor should give instruction in good fishing practices.

HORSEBACK RIDING

Riding at camp can be hazardous, but with adequate safeguards it adds to camp enjoyment. Campers need to be taught to ride, and the riding counselor will be trained in riding techniques. Horses require special facilities for their handling both during camp and in the winter seasons.

SETTING-UP EXERCISES

These are often used in early morning around the flagpole. Health authorities question their value then, when body vitality is at a low ebb.

FIELD TRIPS

Off-site trips are especially valuable in camps where the site is restricted in facilities or opportunities for specialized activities. These must be well planned and adequately supervised.

FILMS

Some camp directors will not allow a film projector on their site. Others seem to use films as a good way to keep the campers quiet. Films may have a place in camp if they fulfill a worthy purpose, never because of lack of planning for something else.

WORK PROJECTS

Short-term camps or small well-developed camp sites offer little opportunity for campers to build trails, bridges, or new buildings, or do other major jobs that are undertaken in some long-term camps. With imagination each cabin or unit may plan each year some minor improvement which they may add to the camp site.

READING

Each camp should have a library with reference books on camp activities. This may also include choice fiction and Christian publications. Public libraries usually are cooperative in providing books. Comic books are taboo in camp. The cabin counselor can help to interest his charges in better reading. Some introverted bookworms may use reading as an escape from mingling with others and need reading curtailed rather than encouraged.

HANDCRAFTS

Handcrafts are a deep-seated camp tradition, but concerning them the camp program committee needs to ask itself these questions:

1. Why has this particular project been chosen?
2. Is it mere busywork to keep the camper occupied during the hour scheduled for handcraft?
3. Is it creative, allowing the camper to express his own individuality? Or is it a pre-cut kit that needs only a few nails or other unimaginative action to complete?

4. What benefits accrue to the camper in making this?

5. Is this the kind of commercial craft that he does all year at home, at school, at a club?

6. What excuse is there for including it in a camp program?

7. Is it intrinsically valuable, or will it be discarded perhaps even before the camper returns home?

Some camps have deleted from their program all crafts except those made from nature materials. Most have done away with scheduled craft hours when the whole camp is required to spend a specified time at commercial crafts. A craft house open during free time or available for projects that grow out of other camp programs seems better to meet campers' needs.

Probably all these and more have been used at camp: *paper crafts:* papier-mâché, crepe-paper projects, and raffia, spatter craft, blueprinting, silhouettes, kleenex projects, paper cutting, paper folding, finger painting; *woodcrafts:* woodcarving, woodburning, carpentry projects, motto making; *metalcrafts:* aluminum foil, copper enameling, aluminum etching, tin-can crafts, wire forming, tray painting; *scrap crafts:* bottles, spools, phonograph records, boxes, cartons, plastic bottles, plastic fluff, ad infinitum; *crafts using special materials:* plastics, felt, fiber flowers, cork, soap carving, glorified glass, basketry, candle crafts, glitter crafts; *ceramics and plaster casting,* carving, mosaics; *homecrafts:* weaving, embroidery, tatting, knitting, crocheting, jersey loops, needle work; *leatherwork and braiding.*

18. SPECIAL DAYS

FIRST DAY AT CAMP

First impressions are very important. Some camps drag the first day; others begin functioning "full speed ahead" as soon as campers arrive.

Every possible provision should be made so that the first impressions of camp will be happy, positive ones. Special procedures must be set up to care for the inevitable early and late comers.

REGISTRATION AREA

As soon as he arrives, the camper should be checked at the registration area with these details cared for:

1. His registration information is completed.
2. His money is deposited and a record made.
3. He addresses a notification-of-arrival card to his parents.
4. In conference-type camps he is assigned to his classes and chooses his special-interest groups.
5. The doctor or nurse meets each child, receiving his medical examination card, being informed of any special physical limitations, and giving further examination as desired.
6. The camper is directed personally to the proper cabin, which has been well identified in advance.

MEETING THE CABIN COUNSELOR

Taking his camp gear, the camper goes to his cabin and is introduced to his counselor, who is on hand to greet him. The counselor introduces him to others in the cabin group, assigning bed and storage space, and orients him to camp routines. The *Camper's Manual* is given to him and explanation of regulations is made personally.

CAMPER'S MANUAL OR SOUVENIR BOOK

This will include information on all or some of the following:

1. Bounds of the camp and method of leaving camp with permission.
2. Type of dress allowed for each camp event.

3. Attendance at classes and services.
4. Use of camp equipment.
5. Meals and K.P. routine.
6. Camp store and money.
7. Use of grounds and rest rooms.
8. Swimming.
9. Mail arrangements.
10. Retiring time.
11. First day and last day arrangements.
12. Titles of the camp staff, with a place for autographs.
13. Space for autographs, addresses, etc., of camp mates.
14. Camp theme songs or other songs.
15. Camp curriculum material (in conference-type camps).

START OF A GOOD TIME

To ward off homesickness—nearly always present with first-time-away-from-home campers—the first day's program must be filled with interesting activities.

After the camper has settled in, plans should be made for a leisurely trip around the camp, a stop at the craft house to make a name pin (thin twig peeled back to expose wood, upon which are glued macaroni letters and a pin back), perhaps a swim.

The first meal at camp should contain well-liked foods in sufficient quantity, with some extra touch that is appealing, letting the campers know at once that the meals are going to be good. K.P. routine should be established by the evening meal. After campfire or vespers an extra snack may prevent homesickness and help the camper sleep better. Campers who find it hard to adjust to new conditions will find that sleep is a long time coming. However, they must have it impressed on them that camp life requires quiet on their part after taps. Since some will usually want to get up at the first crack of dawn the next morning, they should be warned that all stay in bunks (except for necessary trips) until reveille.

OTHER SPECIAL DAYS

SUNDAY IN CAMP

Sunday should be a special day in an evangelical camp. It should be enjoyable, but different in pace and pattern from normal routine.

An opportunity to sleep later and a tempting breakfast menu will give a good start to a happy day. This may become a dress-up day with a regularly scheduled Sunday-school class session, followed by an outdoor chapel service. Sometimes it is desirable to take campers to a nearby church for Sunday service, making arrangements before-hand with the pastor. A good Sunday dinner will be expected at noon.

In the afternoon activities that are in keeping with the conviction pattern of the sponsoring body may be allowed. A hike ending on a hillside to watch the sun go down while a sack lunch is eaten, or a Galilean service at the waterfront will add to the sacredness of the day.

RAINY DAYS

An occasional rainy day can be really fun, depending upon the degree of pre-planning by cabin counselors and program director. Every staff member should know the plans for coping with rainy days as decided during pre-camp training.

Indoors craft programs may be stepped up, time given for quiz programs, impromptu skits, films, quiet games, indoor relays, cha-rades, storytelling, reading, catching up on personal tasks. Outdoors, if it is a warm rain, wet hikes, swimming in the rain, and scavenger hunts are enjoyable. Care must be taken not to allow chilling.

Much depends upon the attitude of counselors whether or not gloom accompanies rain in camp.

CHRISTIAN COLLEGE DAY

Junior and junior high youth are not too young to be thinking about going to Christian schools. An alumnus or school representa-tive from a denominational institution or an approved Christian school may be the speaker in an all-camp gathering. Promotional material from the institution may be on display in the lodge and on the bulletin board. A recent annual of the school, left where it may be perused, will command much attention. Counselors should seek opportunities to interest their charges in obtaining as much training as possible to be of better service in God's Kingdom.

MISSIONS DAY—WORLD FRIENDSHIP

In evangelical circles missionary education should permeate all phases of Christian education, camping among them. Missionary interest may be kept vital in camps by a special missions day. Missionary speakers give the personal touch that brings reality to the world thrust of the Gospel. A missionary offering, in which campers give IOU's on their funds left in the camp bank, can be credited each year to a particular project, which becomes a camp tradition.

Missions atmosphere may be created by posting photographs, maps, letters from missionaries, addresses of missions pen pals, prayer requests. Flags of other nations, missionary texts on banners, curios that may be handled, books for the library may make their impact felt in creating missionary interest. A missions meal with food from a particular mission field is often a camp highlight. A brief report from "the mission of the day" can be made in chapel daily. Some camps schedule a "white harvest dedication service"; each camper chooses a place on the large map, which becomes his own harvest field marked with a colored flag which he personally places during the service.

FUN DAYS AND EVENTS

Time and space forbid an exhaustive listing of ideas that have added fun to camp. Here are a few:

African Safari	Hat Night (from native materials)
Indoor Beach Party	Visitors' Day
Masquerade Party	Campcraft Tournament
Banquets	Craft Show
Election of King and Queen	Boat Trip
Christmas Day in July	Amateur Hour
Campus Cleanup Day	Counselors' Show
Hobo Supper in a Can	Campers' Show
Sadie Hawkins Day	Moonlight Hike
Indian Day	Music Concert
Backwards Night	Nature Show
Water Carnival	Birthday Parties

LAST DAY AT CAMP

Happy memories of camp will be enhanced rather than marred if a carefully planned routine for closing day is carried through.

Camps whose youngsters must travel long distances before nightfall find it advantageous to close immediately after breakfast; others close following a final Bible class period and morning chapel; some close with the noon meal. Whether or not a new group of campers is coming in to the camp site will help to determine camp closing time. Leaving camp before the stated closing time by any group, staff or campers, is to be strongly discouraged. This disrupts camp morale for the ones leaving as well as for those left behind.

The counselor will help each of his campers in these tasks: to pack his own belongings, checking them against the list brought with him to camp; look over lost and found items in the office; return blankets or other supplies to the camp storeroom; see that he has his Log Book, craft items, bug collection, or other personal souvenirs of camp; sign out at office, stating with whom he is returning home (for protection of the camp); obtain any refund from the camp bank; assist in cabin cleanup, policing of grounds, or other assigned closing-day tasks; fill out camper evaluation sheet, if such is provided.

Besides assisting with these the counselor takes time for a personal farewell with each of his campers, encouraging him to stand by the religious decisions made. He completes the staff evaluation forms and report (follow-up) forms on his campers.

Meanwhile the administrative and programs staff will be completing inventories, preparing materials for storage, filling out their evaluation sheets, assisting in camp cleanup, overseeing transportation of campers.

When the last camper has waved his good-by, the final item is stored, and the last door is locked, the camp director will have mixed emotions. There will be relief, mingled with sadness, that another camp season is over; there will be joy from happy memories and new friendships; most of all there will be thankful gratitude to God —and humility—for the privilege of having a part in the rewarding ministry of Christian camping.

BIBLIOGRAPHY

The following books for further study in the field of camp programming are arranged under each heading in recommended order of purchase for the average evangelical camp. See the exhaustive bibliographies listed in the Appendix for further related publications.

GENERAL PROGRAMMING

Hammett, Catherine, and Musselman, Virginia. *The Camp Program Book*. New York: Association Press, 1951. $5.00. Needed by every camp committee.

MacKay, Joy. *Creative Counseling for Christian Camps*. Scripture Press, 1966. $1.50.

Ensign, John and Ruth. *Camping Together as Christians (A Guide for Junior High Camp Leaders)*. Richmond, Va.: John Knox Press (for Cooperative Publishers), 1958. $1.50.

Special Committee on Camps and Conferences of the Division on Christian Education, NCCCA. *Church Camping for Junior Highs*. Philadelphia: Westminster Press (for Cooperative Publishers), 1960. $1.50.

Turley, Grace. *God Has a Plan, A Counselor's Guide to Junior Camps*. Valley Forge, Pa.: Judson Press, 1961. $1.75.

RELIGIOUS EMPHASIS

Camp curricula for Bible classes are published by several evangelical publishers including Scripture Press, Salvation Army, Pioneer Girls, Light and Life Press (Free Methodist), Gospel Light, Assemblies of God (Cleveland), Beacon Hill Press (Church of the Nazarene).

GENERAL BOOKS ON NATURE

(Countless books are available in this field.)

Audubon Junior Clubs. *Nature Counselors Guide*. New York: National Audubon Society. (Complete program for camp nature study, enrolling all campers with this book and six Golden books included in fee.)

Golden Nature Series: *Birds. Fishes. Flowers. Insects. Mammals. Rocks and Minerals. Seashores. Stars. Trees. Weather.* New York: Golden Press. $1.00, paper; $2.50 cloth, each.

Van der Smissen, Betty and Oswald H. Goering. *A Leader's Guide to Nature-Oriented Activities.* Iowa State University, 1965. $2.95.

Peterson Field Guide Series. 13 Titles. Boston: Houghton Mifflin Company. $4.50 each.

Boy Scout Merit Badge Series. New Brunswick, N.J. 35¢ each.

NATURE CRAFTS

Bales, Robert O. *Creative Nature Crafts. Stepping Stones to Nature.* Minneapolis: Burgess Publishing Company. $2.50 each.

Jaeger, Ellsworth. *Nature Crafts,* Macmillan. $3.95.

CRAFTS (Countless books are available)

Hull, Opal. *Creative Crafts for Churches.* Anderson, Ind.: Warner Press, 1958. $1.95. (Evangelical in emphasis.)

Hammett, Catherine T., and Harrocks, Carol M. *Creative Crafts for Campers.* New York: Association Press, 1957. $7.95.

RECREATION

Cox, Claire. *Rainy Day Fun for Kids.* New York: Association Press, 1962. $3.95.

Eisenberg, Helen and Larry. *Omnibus of Fun.* New York: Association Press. $7.95.

MacFarlan, Allan. *New Games for 'Tween Agers.* $3.00. *More New Games for 'Tween Agers.* $3.50. New York: Association Press.

WATERFRONT

All Red Cross and YMCA materials in this field are recommended. They may be obtained from national or local offices.

Pohndoff, Richard H. *Camp Waterfront Programs and Management.* New York: Association Press. $7.50.

CAMPCRAFTS

Hammett, Catherine. *Your Own Book of Campcraft.* New York: Pocket Books, Inc., 1950. 50¢.

Lynn, Gordon. *Camping and Camp Crafts.* New York: Golden Press, 1959. $1.95.

Mitchell, Viola, and Crawford, Ida. *Camp Counseling*. Philadelphia: W. B. Saunders Company, 1961. $6.25.

CAMPFIRE PROGRAMS

Thurston, LaRue A. *A Complete Book of Campfire Programs*. New York: Association Press, 1959. $5.95.

Eisenberg, Larry and Helen. *Fun with Skits and Stunts and Stories*. New York: Association Press. $2.95.

STORYTELLING

Brown, Jeanette Perkins. *Storytelling in Religious Education*. Boston: Pilgrim Press, 1951. $2.00.

STUDY HELPS

1. What is meant by camp program?
2. Of the five general types of camp program, which do you prefer? Why?
3. What are the advantages and disadvantages of giving awards in camping?
4. What are the major program elements in camping?
5. What specific religious activities would you include in a camp schedule?
6. What are three approaches to nature in camp? Which is used in your camp, or in your ideal camp?
7. What are the ten areas of campcraft as standardized by the American Camping Association? Which are the most appropriate for use in junior and in junior high camping?
8. What are the steps in the Red Cross Water Safety Ladder?
9. What should be the deciding factors in choosing handcraft projects?
10. How may music add to camp atmosphere?
11. How may mission be highlighted in an evangelical camp?
12. As a first-day camper what might you expect?

PROJECTS

1. Construct a camp schedule for a junior or a junior high camp that agrees with your camp philosophy.
2. Plan a two-day rainy-day program for a junior or junior high camp.
3. Write copy for a Camper's Manual.

APPENDIX

ADDRESSES OF VALUE TO CAMP LEADERS

CAMPING ORGANIZATIONS

Secular

American Camping Association, Bradford Woods, Martinsville, Ind. 46151

Canadian Camping Association, 4036 W. 30th Avenue, Vancouver, B.C.

Association of Private Camps, 55 W. 42 St., New York, N.Y. 10036

General Church

Division on Camps and Conferences, National Council of the Churches of Christ in the U.S.A., 475 Riverside Drive, New York, N.Y. 10027

Evangelical

Camp Commission, National Association of Sunday Schools, Wheaton, Illinois 60187

Christian Camp and Conference Association, P.O. Box 3727, Van Nuys, Calif. 91405

CAMPING PERIODICALS

Camping Magazine, ACA address above.

Christian Camps and Conferences, Wheaton, Illinois 60187

Canadian Camping Magazine, 4036 W. 30th Ave., Vancouver, B.C.

PUBLISHERS SPECIALIZING IN CAMPING LITERATURE. Write for catalogs.

All of the above camping organizations.

Association Press, 291 Broadway, New York, N.Y. 10007

Burgess Publishing Company, 426 S. Sixth St., Minneapolis 15, Minn. 55415

Denominational publishers will be able to supply any of the books listed in any bibliography when name of publisher is given them.

ORGANIZATIONS WITH MATERIALS HELPFUL TO CAMP LEADERS. Write for lists.

American National Red Cross, 17th and D Sts., N.W., Washington, D.C. 20006

Boy Scouts of America, New Brunswick, N.J. 08903

Camp Fire Girls, 65 Worth St., New York, N.Y. 10013

Camp Archery Association, 200 Coligni Ave., New Rochelle, N.Y. 10801

Girl Scouts of the U.S.A., 830 Third Ave., New York, N.Y. 10022

National Audubon Society, 1130 Fifth Ave., New York, N.Y. 10028

National Council of YMCA, 291 Broadway, New York, N.Y. 10007

National Recreation and Park Association, 1700 Pennsylvania, N.W., Washington, D.C. 20006

National Rifle Association, 1600 Rhode Island Ave., N.W., Washington, D.C. 20036

Outdoor Education Association, Inc., Southern Illinois University, Carbondale, Illinois 62903

Superintendent of Documents, U.S. Government Printing Office, Washington, D.C. 20204

CAMPING BIBLIOGRAPHIES

At the end of each section of this volume is a selective bibliography, listing only a few of the many resources available to camp leaders in each of the fields treated in this volume. Exhaustive bibliographies have been prepared by various groups. Each camp committee should obtain these camp bibliographies for the camp library as well as catalogs from the organizations listed above.

American Camping Association, *Bibliography of Studies and Research in Camping and Outdoor Education* (listing of theses and research by scholars), 60¢.

———, *Cumulative Index to Camping* Magazine. 35¢.

Camp Commission, National Sunday School Association, *Bibliography for Christian Camping*, 1962. 50¢.

———, *Evangelical Camp Resources*, 1962. 50¢.

Joy, Barbara Ellen, *Annotated Bibliography on Camping*, Minneapolis: Burgess Publishing Company, 1963. $2.50

National Recreation and Park Association, *A Guide to Books on Recreation.* An annual edition, free on request.

The Methodist Church. *Camp Bibliography.* Nashville, Tenn. Methodist Publishing House. Free on request.

OUTLINE FOR TEACHING LEADERSHIP AND SERVICE TRAINING COURSE USING THIS TEXT

The student should come to class with the assigned reading done and written answers to questions concerning this portion found in Study Helps at the end of each chapter. This will allow the teacher to present additional material from the bibliographies and help the student to be able to discuss intelligently the most important sections of the assignment.

Ten Sessions

Session One: Part I, Development of Camping
Session Two: Part I, Definition of Camping
Session Three: Part II, Philosophy and Objectives
Session Four: Part III, Administration—to Health Organization
Session Five: Part III, Health Organization to end of chapter
Session Six: Part IV, Camp Site, Facilities, Sanitation, Safety
Session Seven: Part V, The Camper
Session Eight: Part V, The Staff
Session Nine: Part VI, Program—to Nature in Camp
Session Ten: Part VI, Nature in Camp to end of chapter

INDEX

INDEX

Format by Gayle A. Jaeger
Set in Linotype Caledonia